Terry Hawkin

WHEN IN GERMANY

A holidaymakers guide to the language and the country

Language consultant Gisela Moulds

Thanks also to the Goethe-Institut, York

BBC BOOKS

This book accompanies the BBC television series *When in Germany*, first broadcast on BBC 2 in July 1991 (produced by Helen Eisler and Tony Roberts), and the radio series of the same name, first broadcast on Radio 5 in July 1991 (produced by Iris Sprankling).

Published to accompany a series of programmes prepared in consultation with the BBC Educational Broadcasting Council.

All photos © Achim Sperber

Published by BBC Books, a division of BBC Enterprises Ltd, Woodlands, 80 Wood Lane, London W12 0TT

First published 1991

Text © Terry Hawkin 1991

Format © BBC Enterprises Limited

ISBN 0 563 36172 7

Set in 9 on 10½ point Century Schoolbook by Ebenezer Baylis & Son Ltd, Worcester

Printed and bound in Great Britain by Ebenezer Baylis & Son Ltd, Worcester
Colour separations by
Ebenezer Baylis & Son Ltd, Worcester
Cover printed by Richard Clay Ltd, St Ives Plc

CONTENTS

ABOUT THIS BOOK

- If . . .
— you're planning to go to Germany, either as a tourist or on business
— you feel you'd like to have a go at the language
— you'd like at the same time to learn something of the people and their country
. . . then *When in Germany . . .* is for you.

- The book starts with
— facts about Germany and the Germans
— information about the German language and a simple guide to pronunciation
— a starter pack of useful words and phrases.

- At the back of the book you'll find
— a very basic grammar
— word-lists to expand the vocabulary found in the **Lektionen**
— numbers, days of the week and months of the year
— the answers to **Now Try It Out** and **Quiz**
— a German to English word-list.

- The book can be used either alongside the BBC TV and radio series of the same name, or independently as a pocket-sized guide on your travels.

There are fifteen **Lektionen**, each dealing with a common situation that you as a visitor might find yourself in, such as looking for accommodation, getting something to eat or drink, or dealing with problems. They can be tackled in any order, though you may prefer to work your way through from beginning to end.

HOW TO USE IT

- Each **Lektion** is in six parts:

1 **When in Germany . . .** introduces the topic, and gives you the very basic minimum language to get by.
2 **Action** expands this, and considers what else you may want to say by presenting a number of fuller dialogues.

3 Replay explains a little of how the language works.

4 Now Try It Out gives you opportunities to practise what you've learned.

5 Nice To Know presents interesting sidelights on aspects of Germany and the Germans.

6 Quiz contains wordgames and puzzles based on the language of the **Lektion**.

WHEN IN GERMANY ... cassette

Conversations including the language from this book, and from the TV and radio series, are to be found on one C90 cassette, together with opportunities to practise your German and tips on pronunciation.

DO'S AND DON'TS

DO

— remember that the important thing is to get your message across
— use 'body-language' – your hands and the expression on your face – to get over or reinforce what you're trying to say
— have a go!

DON'T

— worry about the mistakes you make or the fact that your accent is less than perfect
— be embarrassed – besides warming to you because you're making the effort, the Germans won't even notice a lot of what you get wrong
— get discouraged – Nobody expects you to get it all right at once

GERMANY AND THE GERMANS

Germany has rarely remained the same shape for long. Having no natural frontiers to the north, north-west and east, and with nine neighbours, its size has varied according to gains and losses in war. Consequently, pockets of German-speakers are found in France and Belgium, Poland and Czechoslovakia.

The most drastic re-structuring came about in 1949 with the cobbling together of the three western zones, occupied by the United States, Great Britain and France, into the Federal Republic of Germany, and the re-titling of the Russian zone as the German Democratic Republic. Yet within a generation the so-called **Wirtschaftswunder**, or economic miracle, had been achieved, and West Germany was on its way to becoming what it is today, the richest and most powerful country in Europe, with a standard of living second to none, and an industrial, economic and educational role-model.

In 1990, the Federal Republic, which was already the strongest country in Europe, with 62 million people living in nearly 250 000 square kilometres of territory, was joined by the 17 million inhabitants of the former Democratic Republic, and their 110 000 square kilometres of land. What does the future hold in store?

And how are we to regard the new Germany? Do we perceive an industrial and economic giant towering over central Europe, gazing hungrily at the smaller fry all around? Is the EC a German attempt to achieve by peaceful means what they failed to achieve in the war?

And do easy-going Bavarians, phlegmatic Westphalians and thrifty Swabians still stride proudly over a patchwork of forests and rivers and romantic towns, where 'oompah' bands play to thigh-slapping **Lederhosen**-clad **Sauerkraut**-eaters? *When in Germany . . .* introduces a rather different picture.

THE GERMAN LANGUAGE

German is the mother tongue of more than 100 million people, coming seventh in the table of world languages, after Chinese, English, Spanish, Russian, Arabic and Portuguese. It's the official language of Germany, Austria, Liechtenstein, and one of the official languages of Switzerland. Thirteen million native speakers live elsewhere, including nearly 5 million in the USA, where one-sixth of the population are of German descent. It's also a second language in the USSR, countries in the former eastern bloc and South America. Every tenth book published is in German, and after English and French it's the language most frequently translated into others.

A ROUGH GUIDE TO GERMAN PRONUNCIATION

It's impossible to give on the printed page more than a brief description of how German is pronounced. The best advice is to listen to the *When in Germany . . .* cassette – and imitate. What follows are merely hints. English words with similar sounds are given, but they are only approximate. German vowel sounds are more akin to northern English vowels than those in standard southern English.

1 Vowels

	SHORT		LONG	
	English	German	English	German
a	fat	**Tasse**	rather	**Sahne**
ä	met	**Kännchen**	mate	**Käse**
e	pet	**elf**	late	**Tee**
i	bit	**mit**	me	**Musik**
o	lost	**Post**	most	**wo**
ö	[1]	**Köln**	[1]	**schön**
u	put	**Butter**	soon	**gut**
ü	[1]	**dünn**	[1]	**grün**

First put your lips in a position to say 'oo'

— for short **ö** say 'e' as in 'set'
— for long **ö** say 'e' as in 'her'
— for short **ü** say 'i' as in 'bit'
— for long **ü** say 'ee' as in 'beet'

NB A vowel before a double consonant is short: **ist**
A vowel before a single consonant is long: **gut**
A double vowel is long: **Tee**
Tee ist gut

2 Diphthongs

	ENGLISH	GERMAN
au	now	**Frau**
äu	toil	**Fräulein**
eu	toil	**Deutsch**
ei	mine	**Wein**
ie	seen	**Wien**

3 Consonants

	ENGLISH	GERMAN
ch	²	**noch, ich**
chs	box	**sechs**
s³	was	**so**
sch	shush	**Flasche**
sp	mash peas	**sprechen**
st	mushed	**Stück**
ß	mass	**Faß**
v	four	**vier**
w	vile	**weil**
z	pizza	**zu**

² No English equivalent. After **a, o, u** and **au** try for the 'ch' in the Scottish 'loch'. (Clear your throat first.) Otherwise use the 'h' sound you find at the beginning of 'huge', 'Hugh'.

s corresponds to English 's' except when it's at the beginning of a word, or part of **sch, sp** or **st**

b, d and **g** sound like 'p', 't' and 'k' when they appear at the end of a word: **gelb, Hand, Krug**

Beware the 'Eastindiaroffice': use your glottal stop (the sound produced by suddenly opening or shutting your glottis, which is the opening at the upper end of your windpipe). If you read 'little bottles' as 'li'l bo'ls', you'll have no trouble. Try **Er hat auf der Elbe gearbeitet**. Each of the syllables here is distinct: **Er – hat – auf – der – El – be – ge – ar – bei – tet**.

NOW TRY IT OUT

Ein Kännchen Kaffee mit Sahne.
Köln ist schön.
Ist er in Oberammergau?
Sprechen Sie Deutsch?
Wie viele Veilchen?
Wo ist die Post?
Der Wein in Wien.
Fräulein! Noch ein Bier vom Faß!
Die Butter ist gut.
Vier Stück, bitte.

FIRST STEPS

The most important words for making real contact are those to do with the social niceties:

Bitte	Please
Danke schön/Vielen Dank	Thank you
Bitte schön	Don't mention it/Go ahead
Entschuldigen Sie	Excuse me

Greetings include:

Guten Tag!	Good day/Good morning/ Good afternoon
Guten Abend!	Good evening
Gute Nacht!	Good night
Auf Wiedersehen!	Goodbye

Yes and no:

Ja, bitte	Yes, please
Nein, danke	No, thank you

Good wishes:

Alles Gute!	All the best!
Viel Spaß!	Enjoy yourself!

GET YOURSELF A DRINK

WHEN IN GERMANY ...

Durstig? (Thirsty?) **Kein Problem!** At the very worst, you can get a drink just by going into a **Bar**, **Café** or **Gaststätte** (restaurant), or even a **Biergarten**, **Bierkeller** or **Bierhaus**, and pointing at what you'd like ... On the other hand, the words for drinks are so easy in German –

Bier Kaffee Tee Schokolade Milch Wein Whisky Kognak Champagner Limonade Wasser Mineralwasser Apfelsaft Orangensaft Tomatensaft (**Saft** – juice)

- So just say what you want – and add **bitte** (please).

You and your family stop at a roadside café.

Waiter	**Guten Tag!**
You	**Guten Tag!**
Waiter	**Bitte schön?**
You	(Pointing at yourself) **Bier**, (pointing at your partner) **Kaffee**, (pointing at your child) **Limonade, bitte!**
Waiter	**Ein Bier, ein Kaffee, eine Limonade. Kommt sofort!** (Immediately.)

- And when you want to pay:

You	**Zahlen, bitte!**
Waiter	**Bitte schön!**

ACTION

You don't make clear that it's a large beer you mean, not a small one, and that it's a pot of coffee, not just a cup.

You	**Ein Bier, bitte!**
Waitress	**Ein großes oder ein kleines?** (Seeing you don't understand, she gestures the meaning). **Ein großes, oder ein kleines?**
You	**Ein großes!**
Waitress	**Sonst noch etwas?** (Anything else?)

Friend	**Kaffee, bitte!**
Waitress	(Pointing to a cup) **Eine Tasse, oder** (pointing to a pot) **ein Kännchen?**
Friend	**Ein Kännchen, bitte!**

This time you order some wine – without saying it's a bottle you've decided on – not just a glass – and white wine, not red.

You	**Wein, bitte!**
Waiter	**Rotwein oder Weißwein?**
You	**Weißwein, bitte.**
Waiter	**Möchten Sie** (pointing to a glass) **ein Glas oder** (pointing to a bottle) **eine Flasche?**
You	**Eine Flasche.**
Waiter	**Eine Flasche Weißwein. Kommt sofort!**

Now you want to order the same thing for two people.

| You | **Zwei Bier, bitte, und zwei Glas Weißwein!** |

And if you're very thirsty, you may want another drink.

You	(Gesturing) **Bitte!**
Waitress	**Bitte schön?**
You	**Noch ein Bier, bitte!**

Finally, if you want to know where the toilets are . . .

| You | **Entschuldigen Sie, bitte – wo sind die** |

13

Toiletten? (Die Toiletten, bitte? if you're in a hurry).

Waiter　　**Hier hinein, am unteren Ende des Saales.**

Don't understand? Don't worry – he'll probably point in the direction of **Herren** and **Damen!**

REPLAY

1 Attract the attention of the waiter or waitress by calling **Bitte!** or **Hallo!** and gesturing.

2 The phrase **Bitte schön** is a very useful one. The waiter or waitress may use it both when taking your order, in the sense of 'What would you like?' and when bringing it (There you are). It's also used in response to **Danke schön** to express 'Please don't mention it' or 'You're welcome'.

3 **Ein Bier** means both '*a* beer' and '*one* beer'. **Eine Tasse** means both '*a* cup' and '*one* cup'. The easiest way of knowing whether to use **ein** or **eine** with a word is to try and remember when you first meet it.

4 You may well be given a bill or bar slip, but until you feel happy with numbers, ask people to write down the price or cost of things. How do you do that? Just gesture 'write' – and add **bitte**.

NOW TRY IT OUT

1 You want to order drinks. Attract the waiter's attention.

2 The waiter comes over. What does he ask you? You order a beer and a mineral water.

3 Order a pot of coffee, a beer, and two glasses of red wine.

4 Ask for a large beer, and then ask where the toilets are.

5

You	(Attract the waiter's attention.)
Waiter	**Bitte schön?**
You	(Order a coffee.)
Waiter	**Eine Tasse oder ein Kännchen?**

You	(Say you'd like a pot.)
Waiter	**Sonst noch etwas?**
You	(Order a glass of white wine and two glasses of orange juice. Later. Say you'd like to pay.)

NICE TO KNOW

Two drinks to try are **Sekt**, a sparkling wine which is the German equivalent of champagne, and **Schnaps**, a corn-spirit with no colour and no smell. The blood alcohol limit for drivers in West Germany (the former Federal Republic) was the same as in the UK – 0.8 milligrams per millilitre. In East Germany (the former Democratic Republic) it was 0.0 (zero) milligrams per millilitre. After reunification, a compromise was being suggested of 0.5 milligrams per millilitre. If you want a low-alcohol drink, then you want something **mit niedrigem** (low) **Alkoholgehalt** or **mit wenig** (little) **Alkohol**, or even **ein alkoholfreies Getränk**. Otherwise give the brand name.

QUIZ

1 Thirsty? A fine lot of drinks, you may think. Rearrange the letters to make up their German names.

A A FAT MENS TOT B A FEN RATS NOG
C CHEAP GRAN M D EET E FAKE FE
F FAT FLEAS P G HIM CL H IS WINS WEE
I KEST J MELON IDA K MINES A WALES RR
L OK GANK M PANS SCH N RAW SES
O SO CHOKE LAD P WET IRON Q WHY SKI

2 All mixed up. Put these statements and questions in the right order to make up a sensible dialogue.

A **Sonst noch etwas?**
B **Ein Bier, bitte.**
C **Eine Tasse oder ein Kännchen?**
D **Guten Tag! Bitte schön?**
E **Ein Kännchen.**
F **Ein großes oder ein kleines?**
G **Zahlen, bitte!**
H **Ein kleines.**
I **Ja! Kaffee, bitte!**

INFORMATION NEEDED

WHEN IN GERMANY ...

If you want **Information** about a town, you'll find it at the **Fremdenverkehrsamt** (Tourist Information Office).

* It's a pleasant surprise to discover how many words used by the Germans are like English ones.

**eine Apotheke   eine Bank   eine Bäckerei   ein Café
ein Fischladen   ein Hotel   der Marktplatz
eine Parfümerie   die Polizei   die Post
ein Restaurant   ein Supermarkt   ein Telefon**

* So which would you ask for if you wanted to

have a coffee?   have a good meal?   buy provisions for the week?   buy some stamps?   get fresh food and vegetables cheap?   buy some Alka Seltzer?   make a phone call?   get some perfume?   buy some bread?   buy some fish?   spend the night?   change some money?   find a policeman?

Remember to add **bitte** – and smile!

- Where's the Tourist Information Office?

You **Wo ist hier das Fremdenverkehrsamt, bitte?**

Passer-by **Das Fremdenverkehrsamt?** (Pointing.) **In der Aachenerstraße. Hier rechts.**

- Most people point when giving directions. In addition, they'll use

rechts (right)   **links** (left)   **geradeaus** (straight on)

You **Ein Supermarkt, bitte?**
Lady **Hier geradeaus, und links.**

ACTION

Three people are standing at the spot marked ●. One wants to change some traveller's cheques, one would like to buy some bread and the third needs some aspirin.

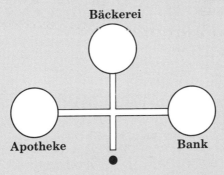

When they ask the way, they are told the following:

A **Hier geradeaus, und dann gleich links.**
B **Gehen Sie geradeaus – immer geradeaus! Da finden Sie eine!**
C **Na ja, hier geradeaus, und dann gleich nach rechts.**

What is wanted by A, B and C?

You're in Lübeck, on business. In the **Fremdenverkehrsamt** you overhear three other visitors. What does each one want?

First Visitor	**Ich hätte gern eine Hotelliste, bitte.**
Second Visitor	**Ich möchte einen Stadtplan.**
Third Visitor	**Haben Sie eine Liste der Campingplätze?**

You want to know what there is to see.

You	**Was gibt's hier in Lübeck zu sehen?**
Assistant	**Die Sehenswürdigkeiten?** (The sights.) **Allerlei!** (All kinds of things.)
You	**Haben Sie eine Broschüre?**

REPLAY

1 Signs are often accompanied by pictograms to make the meaning clear.

INFORMATION   **POST**   **RESTAURANT**

2 The word for 'the' in German takes various forms: **der Marktplatz, die Parfümerie, das Restaurant**. The best way to learn which one to use is to learn it with the word it goes with. Meanwhile, don't worry too much – the important word is the one that follows.

3 When you've discovered that **Ein Supermarkt, bitte?** gets you by, you'll want to try out **Ist hier in der Nähe** (neighbourhood) **ein Supermarkt?** In the same way, you'll expand **Die Post, bitte?** to **Wo ist hier die Post, bitte?**

4 **Eine Apotheke** (apothecary) is where you must go with your prescription. Patent medicines and toiletries can also be had from **eine Drogerie**.

5 If you want to say 'I'd like . . .' then you can use either **Ich hätte gern . . .** or **Ich möchte . . . Ich hätte gern eine Hotelliste. Ich möchte einen Stadtplan.**

NOW TRY IT OUT

1 You're standing on the spot marked ●. Which of these is correct?

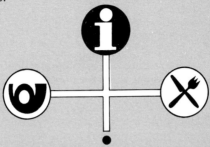

A **Das Postamt? Gehen Sie hier immer geradeaus.**
B **Geradeaus und dann nach rechts. Da finden Sie ein gutes Restaurant.**
C **Sie wollen das Fremdenverkehrsamt? Hier geradeaus, und dann nach links.**

Correct those which are wrong.

2 Auf der Straße

You	(Say 'Excuse me, where's the Tourist Information Office here?')
Assistant	**In her Königstraße. Hier geradeaus. Die erste links.**
You	(Say 'Thank you'.)
Dame	**Bitte schön!**

3 Im Fremdenverkehrsamt

Assistant	**Guten Tag! Bitte schön?**
You	(Wish him good day and say you'd like a list of hotels.)
Assistant	**Bitte schön! Sonst noch etwas?**
You	(Ask what there is to see here in Hamburg.)
Assistant	**Allerlei!**
You	(Ask him if he has a brochure.)
Assistant	**Natürlich! Bitte schön!**
You	(Thank him.)

NICE TO KNOW

The German language is rich in big words formed by putting together two or more smaller ones. It's useful to know this when trying to work out what words mean. **Markt** is 'market', giving us **Supermarkt** and **Marktplatz**; add **Laden** (shop) to **Obst** (fruit) for **Obstladen** or to **Fisch** to make up **Fischladen**, a fishmonger's. **Amt** = 'office'. So what's **ein Postamt**? **Fremdenverkehrsamt** is made up of **fremd** (strange, foreign) + **Verkehr** (traffic) + **Amt** (office). What would you expect to see in the **Nürnberger Verkehrsmuseum**?

QUIZ

1 Pair them up. From the list of words on the right, choose one that will join up with both words in each pair on the left, in order to make up new words. What do the new words mean in English?

1 **SUPER / BUTTER**
2 **MARKT / CAMPING**
3 **FISCH / OBST**
4 **BIER / KINDER**
5 **WEIß / ROT**
6 **WEIN / WASSER**

A **LADEN**
B **GARTEN**
C **GLAS**
D **MARKT**
E **PLATZ**
F **WEIN**

2 All squashed up. Split up this telescoped conversation, firstly into words, and then into phrases and sentences, adding the appropriate punctuation and capital letters. Then arrange it as a sensible conversation.

**gutentaggutentagwasgibteshierinnürnbergzusehen
bitteschöneinelistedersehenswürdigkeitensonst
nochetwasichhättegerneinelistedercampingplätze**

SOMEWHERE TO STAY

WHEN IN GERMANY ...

Although there's no official classification of hotels in
Germany, you'll find a good range of quality
accommodation. The usual word to look for is the
international one, **Hotel**. You'll also find **Hotel garni**,
where breakfast will be offered, but no other meals. Then
there's **eine Pension**, **ein Gasthaus** or **Gästehaus** –
equivalent to a boarding house – and **ein Gasthof**
(country inn or tavern). Don't confuse this with **eine
Gaststätte** – a restaurant or place to eat and drink. The
price you pay is usually for the room, not per person, and
charges, VAT included (**Mehrwertsteuer enthalten**)
will be found displayed in your room.

● You enter a hotel and go to reception – **Empfang** –
where you ask if they have a room for one night.

Receptionist	**Guten Abend!**
You	**Guten Abend! Haben Sie ein Zimmer frei, bitte?**
Receptionist	**Für wie lange?**
You	**Für eine Nacht.**
Receptionist	(Handing you a key). **Bitte schön! Ihr Schlüssel. Zimmer Nummer 45 (fünfundvierzig).**
(Next morning)	
You	**Meine Rechnung, bitte.**
Receptionist	(Handing you your bill) **Bitte schön! Ihre Rechnung.**

● If you stop not in a **Hotel** but on a **Campingplatz**,
much of the language you'll need is the same, but note:

Have you space? **Haben Sie Platz frei?**
Saying whether you have a tent or a caravan – **Wir
haben ein Zelt/einen Wohnwagen.**
And if you're asked **Wie viele Personen?**
Zwei Erwachsene und drei Kinder – two adults and
three children.

ACTION

You want to stop four nights. What does it cost?

You	**Guten Abend! Haben Sie ein Zimmer frei, bitte?**
Receptionist	**Für wie viele Nächte?**
You	**Vier. Was kostet das?**
Receptionist	**Siebzig** (70) **Mark pro Nacht.**

And you may need more than just one single room.

Receptionist	**Wie viele Zimmer brauchen Sie?**
You	**Drei.**
Receptionist	**Einzelzimmer oder Doppelzimmer?**
You	**Zwei Einzelzimmer und ein Doppelzimmer.**

Do the rooms have a bath, or a shower?

You	**Mit Bad?**
Receptionist	**Nein, mit Dusche.**

And you want to know if breakfast is included.

You	**Ist das mit Frühstück?**
Receptionist	**Nein, leider nicht. Ohne Frühstück. Das Frühstück kostet sieben Mark extra.**

At busy times you may be unlucky, of course.

You	**Haben Sie ein Zimmer frei, bitte? / Haben Sie Platz?**
Receptionist	**Ich bedaure, nein. Alles besetzt.**

If only you'd booked!

Receptionist	**Guten Abend!**
You	**Ich habe eine Reservierung.**
Receptionist	**Ihr Name, bitte?**
You	**Smith.**

REPLAY

1 It's likely you'll arrive at your hotel in the evening and be greeted with **Guten Abend!** But it could be in the morning (**Guten Morgen!**) or the afternoon (**Guten**

Tag!). Wish people **Gute Nacht!** only at bed-time.

2 There are several ways of making the plural in German. Learn those you may need as you meet them. **Eine Nacht – zwei Nächte, ein Zelt – zwei Zelte, ein Zimmer – zwei Zimmer**. Only a few words, mostly international ones, take **-s. Zwei Hotels**.

3 When someone wants to know how long you want to stay, they'll ask either **Für wie lange?** (For how long?) or **Für wie viele Nächte?** (For how many nights?).

4 **Leider** (unfortunately) and **ich bedaure** (I'm sorry) are two useful ways of expressing regret.

5 In this **Lektion** you meet **Ihr** (your) and **mein** (my). **Ihr Schlüssel – mein Schlüssel**. Sometimes they have the form **Ihre** and **meine. Ihre Rechnung, meine Rechnung**. But don't worry if you say the wrong one. You'll still get your key – and your bill!

NOW TRY IT OUT

1 Im Hotel

Receptionist	**Guten Tag!**
You	(Wish the receptionist 'Good afternoon', and ask if she has rooms available.)
Receptionist	**Ja, natürlich. Was für Zimmer möchten Sie?**
You	(Say 'Two double rooms and a single, with shower'.)
Receptionist	**Für wie viele Nächte?**
You	(Say it's for two nights and ask what it costs.)
Receptionist	**Ein Doppelzimmer kostet hundert Mark pro Nacht und ein Einzelzimmer kostet achtzig.**
You	(Ask if breakfast is included.)

2 Auf dem Campingplatz

You	(Wish the warden 'Good evening', and ask if he has space.)
Warden	**Ja. Für wie lange?**
You	(Say it's for one night.)

Warden	**Und wie viele Personen, bitte?**
You	(Say three adults and two children.)
Warden	**Haben Sie einen Wohnwagen?**
You	(Say no, you have three tents.)
Warden	**Gut. Ihr Name, bitte?**
You	(Give your name.)

NICE TO KNOW

Hotel language tends to be international. Look out for signs that indicate **RESTAURANT, BAR, LIFT** or **TOILETTEN**. A hotel breakfast can be quite an experience. Start with **Orangensaft**, followed by **Muesli** or even **Corn-Flakes**, and then move on to **Schinken** (ham), **Käse** (cheese) or possibly **ein gekochtes Ei** (a boiled egg) with your **Brot und Butter**, followed by **Marmelade**. Drink it down with **Schokolade, Kaffee (mit oder ohne Milch und Zucker)** or **Tee (mit Milch oder Zitrone)**.

QUIZ

1 A lost letter. One letter – the same one – is missing from the following words. Which letter is it? Can you put it back wherever it should appear?

A **HOTL** B **PNSION** C **MPFANG** D **RCHNUNG** E **DUSCH** F **FRI** G **SCHLÜSSL** H **WOHNWAGN** I **ZLT** J **INZLZIMMR** K **DOPPLZIMMR** L **BSTZT** M **RSRVIRUNG** N **RWACHSN** O **KINDR**

2 Mr Smartt. Here's someone who knows all the answers – but gives them to the wrong questions.

1 **Für wie lange?** A **Zwei Erwachsene und ein Kind.**
2 **Wie viele Personen?** B **Drei Nächte!**
3 **Ihr Name, bitte?** C **Leider nicht!**
4 **Wie viele Zimmer brauchen Sie?** D **Smartt, Alec.**
5 **Haben Sie eine Reservierung?** E **Zwei!**

Which answer should go with which question?

A SNACK

WHEN IN GERMANY ...

What's on offer at the **Schnellimbiß**? Well, if you don't
want a **Hamburger**, you could try a **Frankfurter**, or get
yourself **eine Bratwurst, eine Bockwurst** or even a
highly seasoned **Currywurst**. And if you don't know
what to ask for? Just say **Einmal das, bitte!** – One of
those, please!
● You find the smells wafting from a **Schnellimbiß**
irresistible.

Stallholder	**Bitte schön?**
You	(pointing at a **Bratwurst**) **Einmal, bitte!**

● Would you like French fries with it?

Stallholder	**Mit Pommes frites?**
You	**Ja, bitte!**

● And do you want mayonnaise, ketchup or mustard?

Stallholder	**Mit Mayo? Ketchup? Senf?**
You	**Senf, bitte!**
Stallholder	**Fünf Mark zwanzig!** (5,20 DM)

ACTION

An ice-cream for afters? Go into an **Eisdiele**, and choose:
Vanille, Schokolade, Mokka or **Karamel**. Or one that's
fruit-flavoured? Choose from **Zitrone, Erdbeer**
(strawberry), **Aprikose, Banane, Heidelbeer** (bilberry),
Himbeer (raspberry) or **Kiwi**.

Assistant	**Guten Tag! Bitte schön?**
You	**Einmal Vanille, bitte.**

But what size? The choice is either normal – or big!

Assistant	**Möchten Sie eine normale Portion, oder eine große?**
You	**Eine große!**

The Gelateria Conti in Wuppertal offers:

Kinderportion 2,20   Normale Portion 3,30
Große Portion 4,40   Riesenportion 5,50

das Kind – the child   **der Riese** – the giant

If you want, you can have it with whipped cream.

Assistant	**Mit Sahne?**
You	**Ja, bitte!**
Assistant	**Eine große Portion Vanilleeis mit Sahne. Bitte schön!**

You're with some German guests, this time in an **Eisdiele** that offers small portions. That's not for you though.

Assistant	**Bitte schön?**
You	**Für mich eine Riesenportion Erdbeer-Eis mit Sahne. Und für Sie, Herr Wetzel?**
Herr Wetzel	**Für mich eine kleine Portion Mokka-Eis, bitte.**
Assistant	**Mit Sahne?**
Herr Wetzel	**Nein. Ohne Sahne.**
You	**Und für dich, Wendelin?**
Wendelin	**Für mich auch eine kleine Portion Mokka-Eis, ohne Sahne.**
Assistant	**Einmal Erdbeer-Eis mit Sahne, zweimal Mokka-Eis, ohne Sahne.**

A favourite afternoon occupation is to enjoy **Kaffee und Kuchen** in a **Café-Konditorei**, where you might choose from cakes such as **Obstkuchen, Käsekuchen, Apfelkuchen** and **Schokoladenkuchen**, and tarts and flans like **Sahnetorte, Erdbeertorte** and **Himbeertorte**, including the gateau from the Black Forest, **Schwarzwälder Kirschtorte**. (And all **mit Sahne**, if you want!)

Waitress	**Bitte schön?**
You	**Ein Stück Apfelkuchen mit Sahne, und zwei Stück Erdbeertorte ohne Sahne, bitte.**
	ein Stück – a piece

REPLAY

1 Mal means time, occasion. Put a number in front of it when you want to say once, twice, three times – or more.

Einmal, zweimal, dreimal, viermal, fünfmal . . .

2 Möchten Sie eine normale Portion oder eine große?
The easiest way of answering this is simply to say **Eine große**, but you could add **Ich möchte.**

Ich möchte eine große – I'd like a big one.

3 Another simple way to say what you'd like to eat or drink is to use **für**.

Für mich – for me

Für Sie and **für dich** both mean 'for you'. Use **für dich** when you're talking to a friend, relative, child, or animal.

NOW TRY IT OUT

1 Order, for you and a friend, a **Bratwurst** with French fries and mayonnaise.

2 Im Schnellimbiß

Colleague	**Was möchten Sie?**
You	(Say a **Frankfurter**.)
Colleague	**Mit Ketchup?**
You	(Say no, with mustard.)

3 In der Café-Konditorei

Waitress	**Bitte schön?**
You	(Order three pieces of apple tart.)
Waitress	**Mit Sahne?**
You	(Say two with cream and one without.)

NICE TO KNOW

German sausage can provide not only a gastronomic experience, but also invaluable pronunciation practice. Try **Bierwurst, Jagdwurst, Zungenwurst, Katenrauchwurst, Kalbsleberwurst, Kräuterleberwurst,** or even **getrüffelte Gänseleberwurst.**

If you want a quick, inexpensive, coffee, go to a place like Eduscho or Tchibo, where you stand up to drink it, but a **Café-Konditorei** offers a more meaningful experience. First feast your eyes on the selection of **Kuchen** and **Torten,** ordering at the counter as you go in. When the waitress brings it to your table, order your coffee. Leisurely delectation follows. (Newspapers are provided for those who prefer not to give one hundred per cent attention to the job in hand.)

QUIZ

1 What a mess. We bought a Black Forest gateau, some chocolate cake, a fried pork sausage, a raspberry tart, some strawberry ice-cream and some vanilla ice-cream, but they got in an awful muddle. Here they are:

A WURBS TART B HE HEN LOO DUCK SNACK
C SEE RED BRIE D RAW THRETZ ERRS WITH
SLACK COD E MEETI HERB ROT F VEAL IN LIES

Which is which?

2 A mean menu. Can you suggest any way some of these items could be improved?

A **Bratwurst mit Sahne**	D **Hamburger mit Ketchup**
B **Frankfurter mit Senf**	
C **Sahnetorte mit Pommes frites**	E **Vanilleeis mit Sahne**
	F **Himbeereis mit Mayo**

BREAK THE ICE

WHEN IN GERMANY . . .

Greetings tend to be accompanied by a handshake.
Although younger people may be less formal, it may take
a little longer before older Germans consider themselves
on first-name terms with you. Wait until they use your
first name before using theirs. Meanwhile address a man
as **Herr** . . . , a woman as **Frau** . . . and a girl under 20 as
Fräulein . . . .

• A colleague responds to your greeting, and asks you how
you are.

You	**Guten Tag, Frau Müller!**
Frau Müller	**Guten Tag! Wie geht's, Herr Wood?**
You	**Danke, gut!**

• And if you want to ask 'How are you?' in return:

Frau Müller	**Wie geht's?**
You	**Danke, gut! Und Ihnen?**

ACTION

It's usual to state your name when you're being formally
introduced, but you may want to tell someone who you
are without waiting for an introduction.

Jeff	**Guten Tag! Ich bin Jeff Cook.**
Klaus	**Und mein Name ist Lüdecke, Klaus.** **Guten Tag!**

Where do they both come from?

Jeff	**Ich bin aus Leeds. Und Sie?**
Klaus	**Ich bin aus Berlin.**

Four businessmen are getting to know each other.

George	**Mein Name ist George. Ich bin Engländer, aus Birmingham.**
Scott	**Mein Name ist Scott. Ich bin Amerikaner, und ich bin aus New York.**

| Donald | Ich bin Donald. Ich bin Schotte, aus Glasgow. |
| Jürgen | Und ich heiße Jürgen. Ich bin Deutscher, aus Lübeck. |

And if you don't catch what you're told? On a course for young engineering students, Debra joins Udo for breakfast.

Debra	Guten Morgen!
Udo	Guten Morgen! Wie geht's?
Debra	Danke, gut! Und dir?
Udo	Danke, gut. Ich heiße Udo.
Debra	Langsam, bitte!
Udo (slowly)	Ich heiße Udo – mein Name ist Udo.
Debra	Ah! Und ich heiße Debra. Ich bin aus London.
Udo	Ah – Engländerin!
Debra	Ja! Ich bin Engländerin! Und du? Bist du Deutscher?
Udo	Ich bin Deutscher – aus München.
Debra	Wie bitte?
Udo	Aus München – auf englisch, Munich! Auf deutsch – München. Verstanden?

REPLAY

1 There are several ways of asking and giving names.

Ihr Name, bitte? Mein Name ist Jeff Cook.
Wie heißen Sie? Ich heiße Jeff Cook.
Wer sind Sie? (Who are you?) **Ich bin Jeff Cook.**

2 By adding **–in** to many masculine words, you can make them feminine.

Jeff ist Engländer. Debra ist Engländerin.
Scott ist Amerikaner. Louise ist Amerikanerin.
Donald ist Schotte. Moragh ist Schottin.
But **Jürgen ist Deutscher. Hanna ist Deutsche.**

3 Some useful language management terms:

Langsam, bitte! Slowly, please!
Wie bitte? Pardon?
Verstanden? Understood?

Auf englisch, bitte! In English, please!
Auf deutsch, bitte! In German, please!

4 **Du** and **Sie** both mean 'you'. As young student colleagues, Udo and Debra address each other as **Du**. You'd also use **Du** when talking to close friends, relatives, animals and children. Otherwise stick to the polite word for you, **Sie**.

5 **Wie geht's?** is a short form of either **Wie geht es Ihnen?** or **Wie geht es dir?** You ask Frau Müller, to whom you say **Sie, Wie geht es Ihnen?** Debra asks Udo, to whom she says **du, Wie geht es dir?**

NOW TRY IT OUT

1 John, from Manchester, and Heather, from Glasgow, meet a girl who tells them **Ich heiße Heike. Ich bin Deutsche. Ich bin aus Hamburg.** How do John and Heather give the same information about themselves?

2 Im Restaurant

Herr Lehmann **Guten Abend!**
You   (Wish him good evening.)
Herr Lehmann **Wie geht's?**
You   (Say fine, thank you. And you?)

3 Im Hotel

Child **Wie heißen Sie?**
You   (Tell him, and say where you come from.)
Child **Mein Name ist Wolfgang.**
You   (Ask him if he's German.)
Child **Ja – ich bin aus Köln.**
You   (Say Pardon?)
Child **Köln – auf englisch, Cologne.** Are you English?
You   (Say 'In German, please!')

NICE TO KNOW

By adding **-er** to the name of a town you get a word to describe one of its inhabitants. After seeing the old Berlin Wall, John F. Kennedy described himself as **ein Berliner**. (Jackie could have called herself **eine Berlinerin**.) You can use the same word to describe things from that town, too. The President would certainly have been invited to drink **eine Berliner Weiße**, a local beer speciality, and to eat a **Hamburger** or a **Frankfurter** or two. Had he been in Frankfurt or Hamburg he could have referred to himself either as a **Frankfurter** eating a **Hamburger** or a **Hamburger** eating a **Frankfurter**.

QUIZ

1 On course? Of course! This is the list of members at an international conference you're attending.

A FRANK TURFER B LENN GRADE
C KIRIE ANN MEAR D REG BURHAM
E LENI NIBERR F UTE FARRN-FRINK
G TED USCHER H MARK REANIE
I NEL GRANDINE J CON STITH K UTE SCHED
I SETH COT M BERNI REL N INA GREHRBUM

Among them there are a man and a woman from each of the following places: America, Berlin, England, Frankfurt, Germany, Hamburg and Scotland. They introduce themselves. Frank Turfer begins: **Ich heiße Frank Turfer. Ich bin Frankfurter**. What do the others say?

2 Some conversation! The two people speaking here got a little tongue-twisted.

> **guten taggu tenta gwieg ehtsg**
> **utdan keund ihnen gutda nkesi**
> **ndsie deuts cherj aichb indeu**
> **tsche richh eißeb orisb ecker**
> **sinds ieeng lände rinja ichbi**
> **nausl ondon wiehe ißens iebit**
> **teich heiße prinz essin diana**

Run all the words together, and split them up, adding capital letters and punctuation again. All will be revealed.

HOW TO SHOP FOR FOOD

WHEN IN GERMANY ...

Ein Picknick? The easiest way to get the food you need is to look for the sign **Supermarkt**. But a better bet for fresh food is to follow the signs to the **Markt**, or **Marktplatz**. When you get there, remember – it's the metric system. **Ein Kilo** = about 2¼ pounds. **Ein Pfund** is half a kilo, so just over an English pound.

● Another advantage of the market is that you only need to point at what you want, and say how much.

Stallkeeper	**Bitte schön?**
You	**Ein Pfund, bitte.**

● But you'd know what **Tomaten** and **Bananen** were, even if you didn't see them. Having eaten **Apfelkuchen** and drunk **Orangensaft**, you'd know what **Äpfel** and **Orangen** were. (**Orangen** are also called **Apfelsinen**.) You may also have had your **Tee mit Zitrone**, and you'll remember having had ice-cream flavoured with **Erdbeeren**, **Himbeeren** and **Aprikosen**. You might even have had a **Pfirsich-Melba**. **Eine Ananas** is a pineapple. Now, what do the pears cost?

You	**Was kosten die Birnen, bitte?**
Stallkeeper	**Zwei Mark** (2 DM) **das Kilo.**

● And has he any cherries?

You	**Haben Sie Kirschen?**
Stallkeeper	**Ja, natürlich! Wieviel?**
You	**Ein Kilo, bitte!**
Stallkeeper	**Drei Mark fünfzig** (3,50 DM), **bitte!**

● But you're unlucky with grapes.

You	**Haben Sie Weintrauben?**
Stallkeeper	**Nein, ich habe keine Weintrauben.**

ACTION

You want some apples. Which ones?

You	**Ein Kilo Äpfel, bitte!**
Stallkeeper	(Pointing) **Diese, oder diese?**
You	(Pointing) **Diese, bitte!**

The stallkeeper starts to put some in a bag, but you stop her. She thinks you want bigger ones.

You	**Moment, bitte! Nicht diese!**
Stallkeeper	(Gesturing bigger) **Größere?**
You	(Gesturing smaller) **Nein, kleinere!**

The strawberries look good. You fancy a few more.

Stallkeeper	**Ein Pfund Erdbeeren. Bitte schön!**
You	**Einige mehr, bitte!**
Stallkeeper	(Adding some) **So?** (Like that?)

But you want less than a kilo of pears.

You	**Einige Birnen, bitte!**
Stallkeeper	**Ein Kilo?**
You	**Nein, weniger!**

Now for some meat. Look for the sign **Metzger** or **Fleischer**. How much ham would you like?

| *Butcher* | **Guten Tag! Was darf es sein?** (What would you like?) |
| *You* | **Ich möchte hundert Gramm Schinken, bitte.** |

Anything else? How about some sliced cold meat?

| *Butcher* | **So . . . Bitte schön. Sonst noch etwas?** |
| *You* | **Hundert Gramm Aufschnitt, bitte.** |

REPLAY

1 If you want some fruit, but not a precise amount, ask for **einige**.

Ich möchte einige Orangen, bitte.

2 To make 'small' smaller, we add **-er**. It's much the same in German. **Klein** – **kleiner (kleinere** – smaller ones), **groß** (big) – **größer (größere** – bigger ones), **wenig** (little) – **weniger**. (NB **viel** (much) – **mehr** (more).

3 If the shopkeeper hasn't got what you want, he may use the word **keine**.

35

Nein. Ich habe keine Himbeeren. No, I have no (= not any) raspberries.

NOW TRY IT OUT

1 Ask for a few bananas.
2 Ask the butcher for 100 g of sliced cold meat.
3 **Auf dem Markt**

Stallkeeper	**Bitte schön? Was darf es sein?**
You	(Ask what the tomatoes cost.)
Stallkeeper	**Fünf Mark** (5 DM) **das Kilo.**
You	(Say you'd like half a kilo.)
Stallkeeper	**Diese?**
You	(Say no, smaller ones!)
Stallkeeper	**Sonst noch etwas?**
You	(Ask if she has any raspberries.)

NICE TO KNOW

Buying food is a good way to learn the words for colours. You'll choose between **Äpfel** which are **rot** or **grün**, and your **Bananen** will be **gelb** (**braun** if they're over-ripe). If the **Schinken** was even slightly **blau**, you wouldn't want it. And for your picnic you'll also need some **Brot**, which can be **weiß**, **grau**, or even **schwarz**, (**Pumpernickel**, the black rye bread that comes ready sliced, wrapped in foil).

QUIZ

1 Find the food. In this market square you'll find (in German) tomatoes, bananas, apples, strawberries, raspberries, apricots, pears, grapes, ham, sliced meats, white bread, grey bread, black bread – and one pineapple!

L	L	T	O	M	A	T	E	N	T	W	I
R	E	H	O	A	B	E	N	T	L	N	N
E	F	K	I	R	S	D	I	E	R	E	E
K	P	E	C	A	B	N	I	H	B	K	R
N	A	N	N	I	H	U	I	U	E	N	E
E	P	A	R	C	N	M	A	F	I	I	E
N	N	N	S	R	B	R	S	R	I	H	B
A	E	F	C	E	T	H	E	E	G	C	D
N	U	U	E	N	N	D	K	P	E	S	R
A	P	R	I	K	O	S	E	N	M	I	E
B	E	E	N	E	K	I	R	S	C	U	H
N	W	E	I	ß	B	R	O	T	E	N	P

Copy out all the unused letters. Split them up to find out what there isn't in the market.

2 Really Smartt. Here's Smartt (Alec) again!

A 'Tomaten sind blau.' B 'Gras ist rot.'
C 'Der Himmel ist gelb.' D 'Bananen sind weiß.'
E 'Pumpernickel ist grau.' F 'Weißbrot ist schwarz.'
G 'Graubrot ist grün.'

Please put him right.

das Gras – the grass **der Himmel** – the sky

GETTING ABOUT

WHEN IN GERMANY ...

Many German cities have an integrated public transport system, in which one ticket entitles you to travel through a given zone by bus, tram, local railway – overground or underground – and sometimes even by boat. You may buy your ticket before boarding – often from a machine – and you cancel it yourself in a machine called an **Entwerter**. Most local public transport is for **Nichtraucher**.

● You've decided to go into town by bus. Which one is it?

You	**Welcher Bus fährt zum Marktplatz?**
Passer-by	**Linie neun.** (9)

● Now buy your ticket. It's enough to give your destination when you're asked **Wohin?** but you can add **einmal** (one or once).

Clerk	**Wohin?**
You	**Einmal Marktplatz, bitte!**

● You may not be alone, of course.

Bus-driver	**Und wohin, bitte?**
You	**Zweimal Marktplatz, bitte!**

● Meanwhile, where's the nearest bus-stop? On the left.

You	**Wo ist die nächste Haltestelle, bitte?**
Passer-by	**Hier, auf der linken Seite.**

ACTION

Where's the bus-stop for the town centre? On the right.

You	**Welcher Bus fährt zum Stadtzentrum?**
Clerk	**Linie zwölf.** (12)
You	**Wo ist die nächste Haltestelle?**
Clerk	**Hier, auf der rechten Seite.**

From now on, you go **zu Fuß.** First to the cathedral. But where is it?

You	**Wo ist der Dom, bitte?**

Passer-by   **Hier geradeaus, und links.**

You discover that the castle's also straight on, and left. But is it the first left, or the second left?

You   **Wo ist das Schloß, bitte?**
Passer-by   **Hier geradeaus, und die zweite Straße links.**

The museum's on the right. But is it the second on the right, or the third?

You   **Wo ist das Museum, bitte?**
Passer-by   **Hier geradeaus, und die dritte Straße rechts.**

Here you are, at the museum. But what are the opening-hours?

ÖFFNUNGSZEITEN	
Montag	Geschlossen
Dienstag	15.00–18.00 Uhr
Mittwoch	15.00–18.00 Uhr
Donnerstag	15.00–18.00 Uhr
Freitag	15.00–18.00 Uhr
Samstag	10.00–12.00 Uhr
	und 14.00–17.00 Uhr
Sonntag	10.00–17.00 Uhr

And today's Monday! **Geschlossen!** So before you set out for the waxworks . . .

You   **Wann ist das Panoptikum geöffnet?**
Friend   **Von elf Uhr (11.00 Uhr) bis siebzehn Uhr (17.00 Uhr).**

REPLAY

1 Because it's **der Bus**, you'd ask **welcher Bus?** As it's **die Straßenbahn**, you'd ask **welche Straßenbahn?** And if you wanted to know which boat? Then you'd ask **welches Boot?** (from **das Boot**). Notice how these endings **-er, -e** and **-es** keep reappearing.
2 Destinations: ask **Welcher Bus fährt zum**

Marktplatz, zum Schloß, zum Museum, but for any place that has a name, use **nach**.

Welcher Bus fährt nach Schwabing? Which bus goes to Schwabing?

3 Gehen and **fahren** both mean 'to go'. Use **fahren** if it's a means of transport, **gehen** when you mean on foot.

Ich gehe zum Bahnhof (railway station). **Der Zug** (the train) **fährt nach München.**

4 If you want to know where something is, the easiest way is to ask **Wo ist . . .?**

Wo ist der Dom? Where's the cathedral?

You can also ask **Wie komme ich am besten zum . . .?** (What's the best way for me to get to . . .?)

Wie komme ich am besten zum Dom, zum Schloß, zum Museum?

With **die** words you use **zur** and not **zum**.

Wie komme ich am besten zur Post?

NOW TRY IT OUT

1 Ask which bus goes to the town centre.
2 Tell the driver you want two to the market-place.
3

Passer-by	**Entschuldigen Sie! Wie komme ich am besten zum Dom?**
You	(Say it's straight on, and the third street on the right.)

4

You	(Ask when the museum is open.)
Friend	**Von elf Uhr (11.00 Uhr) bis siebzehn Uhr (17.00 Uhr).**

You	(Ask which tram goes to the museum.)
Friend	**Linie dreizehn!** (13)
You	(Ask where the nearest tram stop is.)

NICE TO KNOW

The German word **Bahn** means 'way', 'path' or 'track', and Munich is one German town where you'll find a lot of them. You could get there on the motorway, or **Autobahn**, or **mit der Eisenbahn** (iron-way), usually shortened to **mit der Bahn.** We call it a railway. (Get off at **der Bahnhof.**) For the 1972 Olympic Games, they built twenty kilometres of city-way (**S-Bahn**, short for **Stadtbahn**, the suburban railway), and an underground-way, the **Untergrundbahn** or metro – look for the sign **U-Bahn** – to complement the buses and the street-way, die **Straßenbahn**, or tram.

QUIZ

1 Which way's that? Link up each direction with the appropriate symbol.

A	2 >	**Die dritte Straße links!**
B	< 3	**Die zweite Straße rechts!**
C	1 >	**Die zweite Straße links!**
D	< 2	**Die erste Straße links!**
E	< 1	**Die dritte Straße rechts!**
F	3 >	**Die erste Straße rechts!**

2 When? How? Where? Unscramble these coded diary entries. Where's our hero going each day, and how?

A Am STENGDAI fährt er mit dem SUB zum SUEMUM
B Am GREFTAI fährt er mit dem OUTA zum KITUMPNOAP
C Am GRONNTSDAE fährt er mit der BANHU- zum NAZTERMDUTTS
D Am WHIMTTOC fährt er mit der SHAßBERNTAN zum PRAMKLTATZ
E Am NAGTOM fährt er mit der SHAN-B zum MOD
F Am GONNSTA fährt er mit dem GUZ zum SLOCHß
G Am MAGSSTA geht er zu UFß zur STOP

GO BY CAR

WHEN IN GERMANY ...

The motto, **Ich dien'** (I serve) is the key to the sign you find over most filling stations – **Selbstbedienung** (self-service), though sometimes you find it in the form **SB-Tanken**.

- But this **Tankstelle** is **mit Bedienung**. What do you say to get your tank filled up?

Attendant   **Guten Tag! Bitte schön?**
You   **Volltanken, bitte!**

- And what grade do you want? Four-star.

Attendant   **Super, oder Normal?**
You   **Super, bitte!**

- The driver at the next pump wants unleaded.

Driver   **Bleifrei, bitte!**

ACTION

You pull in at the Tankstelle Steigerwald. And it's **mit Bedienung** ...

Attendant   **Guten Abend! Bitte schön?**
You   **Super, bitte!**
Attendant   **Wieviel?**

You're about to say **Volltanken!** but you haven't enough cash for that, and the filling-station doesn't accept **Kreditkarten**. There are two ways round your problem.

You   **Zwanzig Liter, bitte!**

   OR

You   **Für dreißig Mark, bitte!**

Pulling over on to the **Parkplatz**, you have a look round. Signs indicate **Picknickplatz**, even a **Joggingplatz**, and another one **Rastplatz**. (**Rast** – rest). **Wasser** – you know what that means. And **Luft**? Anything to do with

Lufthansa, the airline? And there's that **dien** word again!
Öldienst – Batteriedienst – Reifendienst. Reifen?
Made by Michelin and Pirelli, among others. A driver
pulls in. What can that mean? Up goes the bonnet, out
comes the dipstick . . .

Driver　　**Den Ölstand prüfen, bitte!**

REPLAY

1　**Volltanken, bitte!**　means, fill it up!

If you look in a dictionary, you'll find that **volltanken** is
given as 'to fill up'. Similarly, you'll find **prüfen**, 'to
check', so if you want your oil checking – **Den Ölstand
prüfen, bitte**. You might also need to say **Die Batterie
prüfen, bitte!** or **Die Reifen prüfen, bitte!**
2　Two grades of unleaded petrol are available – **Super**
or **Normal** – but only one grade of leaded – **Super**. And
instead of saying **Normal** when you want 2-star petrol,
you can use the general word for petrol, **Benzin**.
3　**Das macht fünfundvierzig Mark** (That comes to 45
DM) and **Das kostet fünfundvierzig Mark** are
alternative ways of saying what things cost. If you want
to ask what something costs, you can ask either **Was
kostet das?** or **Was macht das?** (What does that come
to?).

NOW TRY IT OUT

1　Ask for twenty litres of 4-star.
2　Say you'd like 45 DM worth of 4-star.
3　Ask for the battery to be checked.
4　**An der Tankstelle**

Attendant	**Bitte schön?**
You	(Ask him to fill it up, please.)
Attendant	**Super?**
You	(Say yes, leadfree.)
Attendant	**Bitte schön!**
You	(Ask what that comes to.)
Attendant	**Das macht fünfunddreißig Mark.**
You	(Ask him to check the tyres.)

NICE TO KNOW

Motorways are often called by the names of the towns they join, though they also have a number. The Hildesheim–Göttingen Autobahn is the A7. **Autobahn** signs are written in white on blue. Lorries are not allowed on motorways at weekends.

Other road signs are black on yellow. These are on Federal roads, whose numbers are prefixed by a B, for **Bundesstraße**, and **Landesstraßen**, state roads, whose responsibility is that of the **Land**. (Remember, Germany consists of fifteen **Länder**, states.)

Speed limits: in built-up areas – 50 kph, unless there are indications to the contrary; outside built-up areas – 100 kph; on the **Autobahn** – usually no limit. Many towns have a synchronised traffic-light system, producing **die grüne Welle**, the green wave. If you keep to the speed indicated, then you won't be stopped at the red lights. **Gute Fahrt!** – Have a good trip!

QUIZ

1 Tongue-tied? At a filling station, you ask the attendant to fill up with lead-free. You ask the price, and ask him to check the tyres. But you don't articulate as well as normally, missing out all the vowels. This is what you say: **Gtn bnd! Vlltnkn, btt! Blfri. Ws mcht ds? D Rfn prüfn, btt.** What did you mean to say?

2 Quality cars. Kev, Ben and Mr Horie all drive German cars. Who drives what? (With a name like that, Mr Horie normally uses initials.)

A KEVS L WAGON   B BEN ZEEDS MERC
C MR KEN BOY HORIES WEE CRATE

TAKING A TRAIN OR PLANE

WHEN IN GERMANY ...

The Deutsche Bundesbahn, the state-owned German Federal Rail system, is known for its efficiency, and the reliability and punctuality of its trains.

• In many railway stations you'll find ticket machines. But what if you don't understand the instructions? It may be easier anyway to go up to the **Fahrkartenschalter** and state your destination.

Clerk	**Wohin, bitte?**
You	**Hamburg, bitte!**

• What if you're travelling with a friend?

You	**Zweimal, bitte!**

•Single or return?

Clerk	**Einfach, oder hin und zurück?**
You	**Hin und zurück, bitte!**

ACTION

You and two friends are travelling to Nuremberg.

You	**Nürnberg, bitte! Dreimal.**
Clerk	**Hin und zurück?**
You	**Nein, einfach.**

Which platform, please?

You	**Von welchem Gleis, bitte?**
Clerk	**Gleis zehn.**

Platform ten? **Danke schön!** The lady after you in the queue has a husband and three children in tow.

Lady	**München, bitte! Zwei Erwachsene und drei Kinder.**

Then you overhear a pompous businessman.

Man	**Berlin. Hin und zurück! Erster Klasse!**

It makes you glad you're travelling **zweiter Klasse**. He hasn't even checked what time the next train is.

Man	**Wann fährt der nächste Zug nach Berlin?**
Clerk	**Um neunzehn Uhr dreißig (19.30 Uhr).**
Man	**Wann kommt er an?**
Clerk	**Um zweiundzwanzig Uhr fünfundvierzig (22.45 Uhr).**
Man	(Noting it down) **Abfahrt – 19.30 Uhr. Ankunft – 22.45 Uhr . . .**

Abfahrt and **Ankunft** . . . They sound like two useful words.

REPLAY

1 German distinguishes between **wo?** (where?), and **wohin?** (where to?) in much the same way as English used to with where? and whither?

2 When booking your train ticket, you can add the word **nach** (to).

Einmal nach Hamburg, bitte! One to Hamburg, please!

3 Knowing that **fahren** is 'to travel' helps you to work out or guess **der Fahrplan** (the timetable), **die Abfahrt** (the departure), **die Rundfahrt** (the tour). You may well want to make **eine Stadtrundfahrt** or two.

4 A few more useful questions when you travel by train:
Muß ich umsteigen? Do I have to change?
Ist das der Zug nach München? Is this the train for Munich?
Ist hier frei? Is this seat vacant?

NOW TRY IT OUT

1 Ask for five to Stuttgart – 2 adults and 3 children.
2 Say you want single tickets, second class.
3 Ask whether this is the train for Cologne (Köln).
4 Ask whether this seat is vacant.
5 Am Fahrkartenschalter

You	(Ask when the next train leaves for Nuremberg.)

Clerk	**Um vierzehn Uhr fünfundzwanig (14.25 Uhr).**
You	(Ask whether you have to change.)
Clerk	**Nein, er fährt direkt.**
You	(Ask from which platform.)

NICE TO KNOW

You may choose to go not **mit der Bahn** but **mit dem Flugzeug**, in which case you may well travel with Lufthansa, one of the world's biggest airlines. You'll find a major **Flughafen** in Berlin, Munich, Cologne/Bonn, Düsseldorf, Hamburg, and also in Frankfurt-am-Main, where the huge modern Rhein-Main airport is at the hub not only of the domestic and freight traffic of Germany, but of Europe. Lufthansa have their headquarters there, flying to the major cities of Germany and the world.

QUIZ

1 Ooops! The answers to these questions don't seem to be quite right.

1 **Wann kommt er an?** A **Zweiter Klasse.**
2 **Einfach, oder hin und zurück?** B **Nein, zweimal.**
3 **Wohin bitte?** C **Hin und zurück.**
4 **Welcher Klasse?** D **Um sechzehn Uhr neununddreißig (16.39 Uhr).**
5 **Einmal?** E **Nach Hannover.**
6 **Wann fährt der nächste Zug nach Hannover?** F **Um achtzehn Uhr fünfundzwanzig (18.25 Uhr).**

Which answer goes with which question? Rearrange the questions and their answers to make a sensible conversation.

2 Some trip! This is the route published for a DB excursion.

BRUGHAM – BLÜCKE – RANHOVEN – SLÜDESFORD – LÖNK – FRUTNAM–IN–FARKAM – TRUGSTATT – RENNBÜRG – NENCHÜM – REBLIN

Which towns will the train really go through?

MEETING PEOPLE

WHEN IN GERMANY

A girl you've met in Nuremberg asks you whether you like the city.

Heike	**Gefällt Ihnen Nürnberg?**
You	**Ja! Nürnberg gefällt mir gut!**

- But you've been in several other places you liked.

You	**Hamburg gefällt mir! . . . und Lübeck gefällt mir! Deutschland gefällt mir!**

- Heike wants to know whether you're on holiday in Germany, but in fact you're here to work.

Heike	**Sind Sie auf Urlaub hier?**
You	**Nein! Ich arbeite hier. Ich bin Photograph.**

- And how long are you staying?

Heike	**Wie lange bleiben Sie in Deutschland?**
You	**Fünf Wochen.**

ACTION

You're sitting in the bar of the Hotel zum Weißen Rössl (the White Horse Inn) when a German guest comes up to you.

Guest	**Entschuldigen Sie – ist hier frei?**
You	**Bitte schön!**
Guest	**Sind Sie auf Urlaub hier?**
You	**Ja. Ich bin auf Urlaub hier.**
Guest	**Für wie lange?**
You	**Zwei Wochen.**
Guest	**Wie gefällt Ihnen München?**
You	**Sehr gut! München ist schön!** (pretty, nice)

At a nearby table, Helmut's chatting up Jane. Supposing he were to ask her what she likes to drink?

Helmut	**Trinken Sie gern Löwenbräu?**

Jane	**Ja, ich trinke gern Löwenbräu . . . Ah! Da ist mein Mann!** (Calls out) Mick, over here! (To Helmut) **Mein Mann ist Ringer . . . der Ringer** – wrestler

Naturally, Jane introduces Helmut to her husband.

Jane	**Mick, das ist Helmut. Helmut, das ist mein Mann, Mick.**
Mick	**Guten Tag, Helmut!**
Helmut	**Guten Tag . . .**
Brünnhilde	(from a distance) **Helmut!**
Helmut	**Das ist meine Frau, Brünnhilde . . .**

REPLAY

1 If you want to say you like something, then use the expression **es gefällt mir** (it pleases me).

Hamburg gefällt mir. I like Hamburg.

2 If you want to say you like doing something, then use the word **gern**, which literally means willingly.

Trinken Sie gern Löwenbräu? Do you like drinking Löwenbräu?
Gehen Sie gern ins Theater? Do you like going to the theatre?

3 Heike asked **Sind Sie auf Urlaub?** You said **Ich arbeite hier** (I'm working here). A third possibility would be **Ich bin geschäftlich hier** (I'm here on business).

4 If someone wants to know what you do for a living, they'll ask you **Was sind Sie von Beruf?** You said **Ich bin Photograph** (I'm a photographer). Notice that the word for 'a' is left out.

Ich bin Ingenieur. I'm an engineer.
Ich bin Ärztin. I'm a (female) doctor.

A male doctor would say **Ich bin Arzt.**

5 Like Jane, you may want to introduce your family and friends, either in person or by showing photographs. Just say **Das ist mein Mann, meine Frau, mein Vater, meine Mutter, mein Sohn, meine Tochter, mein**

49

Großvater, meine Großmutter, mein Bruder, meine Schwester, mein Freund or **meine Freundin**.

NOW TRY IT OUT

1 You're asked **Was sind Sie von Beruf?** What do you answer?

2 You're showing some photographs to a German friend.

You	(Say 'This is my husband. He's an engineer.')
Friend	**Und Sie?**
You	(Say you're a doctor.)

3 You meet a colleague in the bar at your conference.

You	(Ask whether the seat next to him/her is vacant.)
Colleague	**Bitte schön!**
You	(Ask whether he/she likes the conference – **die Konferenz**).
Colleague	**Ja, sehr.**
You	(Ask whether he/she likes drinking Löwenbräu.)

4 In Hamburg, you sit down next to a German tourist.

Tourist	**Hamburg ist schön, nicht wahr?**
You	(Say yes, you like Hamburg.)
Tourist	**Sind Sie auf Urlaub hier?**
You	(Say no, you're here on business.)

NICE TO KNOW

Modern Germans tend to be of a liberal and democratic tendency and of a European mind. They are also ready for the European role: their vision of the future has led to the creation of a system of education and training geared to the needs of the nation. Forty-seven per cent of 16–18-year-olds stay on at school in Germany, compared with 33 per cent in the UK, and 90 per cent of German school-leavers receive vocational training, 72 per cent of them combining a course of further education with work experience.

QUIZ

1 All mixed up. What happens when you're so overwhelmed that you give the wrong answers?

1	*Colleague*	**Entschuldigen Sie – ist hier frei?**
A	*You*	**Nein, ich bin geschäftlich hier.**
2	*Colleague*	**Sind Sie auf Urlaub hier?**
B	*You*	**Ja, ich trinke gern Wein.**
3	*Colleague*	**Für wie lange?**
C	*You*	**Bitte schön!**
4	*Colleague*	**Wie gefällt Ihnen Berlin?**
D	*You*	**Eine Woche.**
5	*Colleague*	**Trinken Sie gern Wein?**
E	*You*	**Berlin gefällt mir gut!**

What should you have said?

2 Mum's the word. Or is it? In this Wordsearch look for the German words for daughter, father, grandfather, grandmother, husband, mother, son, wife, male friend and female friend. One of them is missing. Which one? Copy out the unused letters to find out why you want to keep quiet about this person's job in life.

```
M M U T T E R E R
I N A N E G E E E
R I O N ß M T U T
T D T E N A H R A
S N I E V H C I V
S U T ß R I O N G
E E O R I N T S V
F R A U O N B E R
G F R E U N D U F
```

THINGS YOU MIGHT DO

WHEN IN GERMANY ...

More than one in two Germans go away on holiday at least once a year. Their favourite destinations? **Italien, Spanien, Österreich** (Austria), **Frankreich, Jugoslawien** and **die Schweiz** (Switzerland), though one-third prefer to stop at home in **Deutschland**. What can you do there? Take your choice: **Schwimmen, Wandern, Radfahren** (cycling), **Tanzen, Oper, Park, Theater, Konzert, Disco, Museum, Musik, Zoo, Trinken, Sport** (Squash, Tennis, Reiten, Fußball, Skifahren, Golf, Gymnastik, Athletik, Handball ...)

• To establish whether what you want to do is possible, off you go to the **Fremdenverkehrsamt**.

You	**Kann man hier schwimmen?**
Assistant	**Ja, natürlich. Wir haben ein gutes Hallenbad.**

• After your swim, a little exercise. Where can you play tennis?

You	**Wo kann man Tennis spielen?**
Assistant	**Es gibt einen Tennisplatz im Stadtpark.**

• And after that, a bike ride. Where can you hire bikes?

You	**Wo kann man Fahrräder mieten?**
Assistant	**Sie wollen ein Fahrrad mieten? Bei Müller, in der Brechtstraße.**

ACTION

You and a friend decide to go to Müller's and hire some bikes. How long for?

Herr Müller	**Guten Tag! Bitte schön?**
You	**Wir möchten Fahrräder mieten, bitte.**
Herr Müller	**Ja, für wie lange?**

You're thinking of a week – but what's the cost?

You	Eine Woche? Was kostet das?
Herr Müller	Eine Woche? 55 DM pro Fahrrad. Ist das okay?
You	Okay!

Do you have to leave a deposit?

You	Wollen Sie eine Anzahlung?
Herr Müller	Nein! Ihr Name, bitte, und Ihre Adresse?

REPLAY

1 Notice the odd word-order in phrases like **Kann man hier schwimmen?** (Can one swim here? Literally, Can one here swim?)

Wo kann man Tennis spielen? Where can you play tennis?

NB **Man** doesn't have the kind of snooty tone associated with the English word 'one'.

2 If you want to know whether something exists in a town, ask **Gibt es . . . ?**

Gibt es ein Theater, ein Museum, ein Stadion, einen Tennisplatz?

3 **Im** is short for **in dem**.

Im Stadtpark – in the town park.

4 With street-names you find the word for 'the'.

In der Goethestraße – in Goethe Street.
5 Bei Müller – at Müller's, ie at Mr Müller's shop.
6 If you want to hire some other things:

Ich möchte ein Pedalo, ein Windsurfbrett, einen Liegestuhl (a deckchair), **einen Strandschirm** (a beach umbrella), **ein Paar Skier, ein Paar Skistiefel** (boots) **mieten.**

How long for?

Für eine Stunde (an hour), **zwei Stunden, einen Tag, zwei Tage, eine Woche, zwei Wochen.**

On the beach you might also ask for **einen Strandkorb** – a portable basketwork shelter to sit in to protect you against the breezes from the North Sea!

NOW TRY IT OUT

1 Ask whether there's an indoor swimming pool here.
2 Say you'd like to hire a deckchair and ask how much it costs.
3 Say you'd like to hire a windsurf board for the day and ask if you have to leave a deposit.
4 At the ski hire shop

Assistant	**Bitte schön?**
You	(Say you'd like to hire a pair of skis.)
Assistant	**Ja. Für wie lange?**
You	(Ask what it costs.)
Assistant	**Zwanzig Mark** (20 DM) **pro Tag.**
You	(Say for three days.)
Assistant	**Kein Problem! Ihr Name, bitte, und Ihre Adresse?**
You	(Give your name, and add 'The Pension Friedegg'.)
	(**Friede** – peace + **Ecke** – corner. Nothing to do with breakfast . . .)

NICE TO KNOW

In the Federal Republic there were 40 000 sports grounds, 30 000 sports halls, and nearly 8000 swimming pools, mostly built between 1960 and 1975 with public money. Every third inhabitant was a member of one or more of the 63 000 sports clubs under the umbrella of the German Sports Federation (**Deutscher Sportbund** or **DSB**), millions of people taking part in the DSB **Trimm dich fit** and **Sport für alle** campaigns. Most join in just for fun, or to keep fit, though you can go in for the gold, silver or bronze **Sportabzeichen** (sports badges) awarded by the DSB for passing certain tests of achievement.

QUIZ

1 Not quite right. You get some funny answers in this **Fremdenverkehrsamt**.

1 **Kann man hier schwimmen?** A **Ja, bei McDonalds!**
2 **Kann man hier skifahren?** B **Ja, in der Disco!**
3 **Kann man Hamburger essen?** C **Ja, im Hallenbad!**
4 **Kann man tanzen?** D **Ja, im Stadtpark!**
5 **Kann man Tennis spielen?** E **Ja, in den Bergen!**

Which answer goes best with each question?

2 Nice girls. You meet these young ladies on holiday in Germany. Which country does each one come from?

A Cheri Kranf B Heidi Wescz C Nola Weisguj
D Rösi Certhe E Lena Iti F Nina Pes G Ute Schlandd

KEEP IN TOUCH

WHEN IN GERMANY ...

If you want to phone home, look or ask for **ein Telefon** or **einen Fernsprecher**, marked **International** rather than **National**. (It could also be marked **Ausland** or **Inland**.) When you pick up the receiver a sign lights up asking you to pay (**Bitte zahlen**). Put in coins worth 1 Mark, 50 Pfennig or 10 Pfennig (minimum 30 Pfennig) and dial.

- Suppose you decide to write home instead? Off to a shop that sells postcards.

You	**Haben Sie Postkarten?**
Shopkeeper	**Ja. Bitte schön!**
You	**Was kosten sie?**
Shopkeeper	**Diese? Fünfzig Pfennig** (50 Pf) **das Stück.**

das Stück – the piece ie each

- Having chosen them, you offer to pay.

You	**Diese Postkarten, bitte!**

Shopkeeper	**Wie viele?**
You	**Acht** (8).
Shopkeeper	**Vier Mark** (4 DM).

- What about stamps?

You	**Haben Sie Briefmarken?**
Shopkeeper	**Ja. Wie viele? Acht?**

- All you need now is a letter-box.

You	**Ist hier in der Nähe ein Briefkasten?**
Shopkeeper	(Pointing) **Ja! Da drüben!**

ACTION

- You always find you need more postcards. A different shop this time.

You	**Was kosten diese Postkarten, bitte?**
Shopkeeper	**Neunzig Pfennig das Stück.**

- 90 Pf? Much too dear! Has he no others?

You	**Zu teuer! Haben Sie keine anderen?**
Shopkeeper	**Diese sind billiger – siebzig Pfennig (70 Pf) und vierzig Pfennig (40 Pf) das Stück.**

- That's better! You choose some, but at which price?

Shopkeeper	**Zu welchem Preis?**
You	**Zwei zu siebzig Pfennig und drei zu vierzig Pfennig.**

- This time you get your stamps at the post-office. You've forgotten the price of a stamp for a postcard.

You	**Was kostet eine Briefmarke für eine Postkarte?**
Official	**Wohin?**

- Silly! Where's it for?

You	**Nach England.**
Official	**Eine Postkarte nach England kostet sechzig Pfennig** (60 Pf).

- And don't forget your letter.

You	**Und ein Brief?**
Official	**Auch nach England?**
You	**Nach Schottland.**
Official	**Das ist auch Großbritannien, nicht wahr?**

- Next time just ask for the stamps.

You	**Briefmarken, bitte!**
Official	**Wie viele?**
You	**Zwei zu einer Mark, und fünf zu 60 Pfennig** (60 Pf).
Official	**Zwei Briefmarken zu einer Mark, und fünf zu 60 Pfennig – das macht fünf Mark** (5 DM), **bitte.**

REPLAY

1 When you have to make a choice between things, the easiest way is to point and say **bitte**. If you like, add **Dies!** (this) or **Diese!** (these).

2 How to object to what you're offered:

zu teuer! (too dear) **zu groß!** (too big)
zu klein! (too small) **zu viel!** (too much)
zu wenig! (too little)

3 Nicht wahr? (Isn't that so?) is rather like the French expression **n'est-ce pas?**

NOW TRY IT OUT

1 Ask for three postcards at 60 Pf and four at 50 Pf.

2

You	(Ask what these postcards cost.)
Shopkeeper	**Eine Mark das Stück.**
You	(Say that's too dear and ask if she has any others.)

3

Auf der Post

You	(Ask what it costs to send a postcard to Scotland.)

Official	**60 Pfennig.**
You	(Ask for ten – **zehn** – stamps at 60 Pfennig.)
Official	**Bitte schön.**
You	(Ask if there's a letter-box nearby.)

NICE TO KNOW

Only a few German newspapers have a national circulation. Among them are *Bild*, a tabloid rather like the *Sun*, selling five million copies daily, and *Die Welt*, a daily for the more serious-minded selling 215,000. Many dailies are produced regionally, though some of them, such as the *Frankfurter Allgemeine* and the *Süddeutsche Zeitung*, do circulate nationally. Most bigger towns have their own local newspaper, which can be easier to understand and more fun to browse through. Of the thousands of periodicals, particularly popular are the illustrated magazines *Stern* and *Bunte*, and the weekly news magazine *Der Spiegel*.

QUIZ

1 Some titles! The titles *Bunte, Bild, Welt, Stern, Zeitung* and *Spiegel* are all German words you could find useful. Remove the letters in each of them from one of the rather strange titles that follow, in order to find out the English meaning.

A WWOERLLTD   B COBLUOURNFTUEL
C NZEEWISPTAUPNEGR   D SMPIIRERGOERL
E PBICITLUDRE   F STSETRANR

2 Careful! McTavish articulates badly in German. He said:

CIßLSSHRDU ACS DAIßS BDOHRDU! CIßLSSHRDU
EDU BDOHRDU CADU AD OTLNGTASRDDABD!

Use this code to work out what he meant to say.

A = I	B = E	C = S	D = N
E = U	G = B	H = L	I = C
L = O	N = ß	O = G	R = A
S = T	ß = H	T = R	U = D

A GOOD MEAL

WHEN IN GERMANY ...

If it's a snack you want, an **Imbißstube** or the restaurant of a department store will give value for money; any **Kneipe** (pub) will lay on food; a **Gasthof** (inn) will usually provide **gut bürgerliche Küche** (good plain cooking); otherwise look for a **Gaststätte** or **Restaurant**. The **Ratskeller**, situated under the town-hall, is often a good bet.

- You'll need to ask for a table.

Waiter	**Guten Abend!**
You	**Haben Sie einen Tisch für zwei?**

- When it comes to ordering, you could look at what they're eating on the next table, and say **Einmal das, bitte!** On the other hand, you could look at the menu.

You	**Das Menü, bitte!**
Waiter	**Bitte schön!**

- There are a lot of things you recognise – **Suppe, Omelett, Roastbeef, Fisch, Sauce, Reis, Spaghetti, Filetsteak, Pommes frites, Nudeln, ein grüner Salat** ... Your companion chooses first.

Companion	**Ein Filetsteak und Pommes frites**
You	**Und für mich ein Omelett, bitte.**
Waiter	**Einmal Filetsteak und Pommes frites, einmal Omelett. Kommt sofort!**

- Do you want something to drink?

Waiter	**Und zu trinken?**
Companion	**Ein großes Bier, bitte!**
You	**Und für mich ein Glas Weißwein.**

- All you need now is to ask for the bill.

You	**Hallo! Zahlen, bitte!**

ACTION

You're fed up with steaks and omelettes, and have decided to equip yourself with a few useful words. Firstly **Fleisch** (meat). This gives you a clue to **Schweinefleisch** (pork), **Rindfleisch** (beef) and **Kalbfleisch** (veal). **Hammelfleisch** is mutton, but will probably be referred to as **Lamm**. **Hähnchen** is chicken, though in a posh place you'll find **Poularde**. Some vegetables (**Gemüse**)? How about **Pilze** or **Champignons** (mushrooms), **Bohnen** (beans), **Spinat** (spinach) or **Karotten**? **Kartoffeln** are potatoes, often in the form of **Bratkartoffeln** (fried potatoes). Off to the **Ratskeller** now, with a new-found confidence! You even use the German word for 'menu'.

You   **Die Speisekarte, bitte!**
Waitress   **Bitte schön!**

What's on?

**Paniertes Schweineschnitzel, in Butter gebraten, mit
Pommes Frites** 14,20
**Gefülltes Kalbsschnitzel, mit Käse und Schinken,
auf Gemüsenudeln** 22,00
**Rinderfiletspitzen mit Pilzen, in Armagnacsauce,
dazu grüne Nudeln** 29,50
**Poulardenbrust in Weißweinsauce, mit
Broccoligemüse und Butterreis** 17,50

Another item looks interesting. What can it be?

You	**Zürcher Geschnetzeltes? Was ist das?**
Waitress	**Das ist Kalbfleisch in Weißweinsauce mit frischen Champignons und Bratkartoffeln.**
You	**Einmal das, bitte!**

REPLAY

1 At the beginning of a meal, your host may wish you
Guten Appetit! or **Mahlzeit!** The reply is **Danke,
gleichfalls!** (Thank you. The same to you!).

Some more useful words and phrases:

Schmeckt's? Do you like it?
Lecker! Delicious!
Stimmt so! Keep the change!

2 Notice how the endings **-er, -e** and **-es** crop up again.

**ein grüner Salat   gut bürgerliche Küche   ein großes
Bier**

What's the word for 'the' in each case?

3 Your bill will usually say **inkl. Mehrwertsteuer und
Bedienung** (including VAT and service).

NOW TRY IT OUT

1 Ask the waiter whether he has a table for four.
2 **Im Restaurant**

You	(Call the waitress.)
Waitress	**Bitte schön?**

You	(Ask for the menu.)
Waitress	**Bitte schön!**
You	(Ask what **Ratsherrenschmaus** is.)
Waitress	**Das ist Roastbeef und Schweinebraten auf Graubrot.**
You	(Order a veal Schnitzel with noodles.)
Waitress	**Und zu trinken?**
You	(Order a glass of white wine.)

NICE TO KNOW

Tradition says that Germans may eat five meals a day, besides being nibblers. The first is **das Frühstück**, a light breakfast of rolls, butter, jam, and coffee and tea. **Das zweite Frühstück**, a cheese or meat sandwich taken to work, is eaten in mid-morning. The main meal, at midday, is **das Mittagessen**, possibly soup followed by meat (often pork, sometimes beef or veal, less often lamb or mutton) with potatoes or other vegetables, and finished off with a sweet, which may be fruit or a **Quarkspeise**, a kind of yoghurt. **Kaffee und Kuchen** comes in the course of the afternoon. The final meal is **das Abendbrot**, at about 7 pm, when you make your own open sandwiches from a selection of cold meats, ham, sausage and cheese, with salad, and weak tea or beer to drink. (In fact nowadays many people are into healthy eating and would blanch at such a schedule.)

QUIZ

1 Not quite right. This diner's in such a hurry he runs the things he has to say together – and in the wrong order. Divide what he says into sentences, add punctuation, and rearrange them correctly.

eine Flasche Rotwein die Speisekarte bitte zahlen bitte haben Sie einen Tisch für drei Hallo Kalbsschnitzel mit Nudeln

2 Chopped-up meats. Four kinds of meat here. But which is which? And what's each one called in German?

A FRIED LC SHIN B HIS NEW ICE FLESCH
C LES FLEC HIM HAM D LE BLACK FISH

MEDICAL EMERGENCIES

WHEN IN GERMANY ...

If you're poorly, say **Ich bin krank**, and if you feel sick **Mir ist schlecht** or **Mir ist übel**. If the doctor asks you **Wo tut es weh?** (Where does it hurt?) all you need do is point. Or you could say it in German. After writing all those postcards home, for example: **Mein Finger tut weh**. Most bits of the body should give you no trouble: **Meine Hand, meine Schulter, meine Nase, meine Brust** (breast, chest), **mein Arm, mein Knie, mein Fuß, mein Bein** (leg), **mein Ohr** (ear), **mein Auge** (eye), **mein Mund** (mouth), **mein Zahn** (tooth).

* The doctor asks you what's wrong.

You	**Guten Tag, Herr Doktor!**
Doctor	**Guten Tag! Was fehlt Ihnen?**
You	**Mein Fuß tut weh.**

* He examines your foot. Nothing seriously wrong. He prescribes an ointment, and gives you a piece of advice.

Doctor	**Ich gebe Ihnen eine Salbe. Und bleiben Sie heute in Ihrem Hotel!**

* What? Stop in your hotel? With the **Oktoberfest** starting today? Not likely!

ACTION

If you've a headache, you express it slightly differently.

You (holding your head in your hands) **Ich bin krank, Herr Doktor.**

Doctor **Haben Sie Kopfschmerzen?**

You **Ja ... Ich habe Kopfschmerzen ...**

Is that all?

Doctor **Haben Sie auch Halsschmerzen?**

You **Bitte?**

Doctor (Pointing at his throat) **Halsschmerzen.**

You have a bit of a sore throat, yes ...

You **Ja ...**

Doctor **Haben Sie Fieber?**

You **Bitte?**

Doctor (Taking his thermometer) **... Aha! Sie haben Grippe!**

The flu? But what will the doctor give you for it?

Doctor   **Nehmen Sie diese Tabletten . . .**

And how often do you take them?

Doctor   **. . . dreimal am Tag.**

Yes! The man you had a **Steinkrug** or two with in the beer tent had the flu! He must have breathed germs over you while teaching you to sing 'In München steht ein Hofbräuhaus . . .'

REPLAY

1 There are several words for doctor. If you want someone to ring for one, say **Rufen Sie bitte einen Arzt an.** When **der Arzt** comes, address him as **Herr Doktor.** (If it's **eine Ärztin**, address her as **Frau Doktor.**)
2 **Ihnen** is the form of **Sie** (you) which means 'to you'.

Ich gebe Ihnen eine Salbe   I'll give (to) you an ointment.

It's also found idiomatically.

Was fehlt Ihnen?   What's the matter with you? (Literally, What's lacking to you?)

Similarly, **mir** is the form of **ich** that means 'to me'.
Literal: **Der Arzt gibt mir Pillen.**   The doctor gives (to) me some pills.
Idiomatic: **Es geht mir schlecht.**   It goes badly to me.
3 Some more complaints:

Mir ist heiß (I'm hot)   **Mir ist kalt** (I'm cold)
Ich habe Magenschmerzen (I've got stomach-ache)
Ich habe Zahnschmerzen (I've got tooth-ache – see a
   Zahnarzt)

4 At the **Apotheke** you could also consult the pharmacist about a minor ailment.

Haben Sie etwas gegen einen Insektenstich, Grippe, Durchfall, Verstopfung, Sonnenbrand?
Have you anything for an insect-bite, the flu, diarrhoea, constipation, sunburn?

NOW TRY IT OUT

1 Beim Arzt

You	(Wish him good day.)
Doctor	**Guten Tag! Was fehlt Ihnen?**
You	(Say your nose hurts and you have a temperature.)
Doctor	**Haben Sie Halsschmerzen?**
You	(Say yes, and diarrhoea.)

2 In der Apotheke

You	(Ask him if he has anything for sunburn.)
Pharmacist	**Ja, eine Salbe?**
You	(Say thank you and ask what it costs.)

NICE TO KNOW

If you're **krank**, let's hope you don't need the **Krankenwagen** to take you to your **Krankenbett** in the **Krankenhaus**. What you will need is a **Krankenschein**, or certificate of entitlement to treatment. Before you leave the UK get a form E 111 from the post-office. If you fall ill in Germany, show this at the local AOK (**Allgemeine Ortskrankenkasse**, sickness insurance office) and they'll give you a **Krankenschein** and a list of doctors and dentists who will treat you free of charge.

QUIZ

1 Come again? You're so ill you have difficulty speaking to the doctor. This is what you come out with:

Gtntghrrdktrmrstschlchtchbnkrnkmnbrstttwhndchhb hlsschmrzn!

Restore all the vowels, capital letters and punctuation.

2 Sounds painful. Which ailments are these?

A SCZHLEHRNSEMA B MENS PFECHKROZ
C FULL DARCH D SCHERMENZ MANGE
E HERNZSCHMENZA F VUPFENS GROT

HELP NEEDED

WHEN IN GERMANY . . .

Kaputt, you reflect as you contemplate the broken heel of
your shoe, is one of those German words that everyone
knows . . . But look – there's a **Schuhmacher**! You go in.

Assistant	**Guten Tag!**
You	**Guten Tag! mein Schuh ist kaputt.**

• While the repair's being done, you go to a nearby bank
to change some money.

You	**Guten Tag! Ich möchte Geld wechseln, bitte.**

• Alas! On the way to collect your shoe, you find you've
lost your wallet. Luckily there's a **Fundbüro** nearby, a
lost-property office. You go in and tell them what's
happened.

You	**Können Sie mir bitte helfen?**
Official	**Ja, gerne. Haben Sie etwas verloren?**
You	**Ja! Ich habe meine Brieftasche verloren.**

ACTION

So it's back to the bank. As you've no cash left, you need
to change some traveller's cheques this time.

You	**Ich möchte Reiseschecks wechseln.**
Bank clerk	**Wie viele?**
You	**Zwei zu fünfzig Pfund Sterling.**

As you go out you bump into someone, and your glasses
fall off and break. You're in luck, though! Next to the
bank there's a shop marked **Foto-Optik**.

Assistant	**Guten Tag! Womit kann ich Ihnen helfen?**
You	**Meine Brille ist kaputt.**

Will you have enough money? What will the repair cost?

You	**Was kostet die Reparatur, bitte?**

Panic! The money's gone! Stolen by the man you bumped into just now. But your luck's in again! Just opposite the optician's you see a sign – **Polizei**. You explain that someone's stolen your money.

Policeman	**Womit kann ich Ihnen helfen?**
You	**Jemand hat mein Geld gestohlen!**

When? A few minutes ago.

Policeman	**Wann?**
You	**Vor einigen Minuten.**

And where? You tell him – outside the bank.

Policeman	Und wo?
You	Vor der Bank.
Policeman	Ihr Name, und Ihre Adresse?

As you leave the **Polizeiwache**, a car sprays muddy water on to your coat. But your good fortune knows no bounds today – right next door you see a sign saying **Reinigung**, cleaners . . .

REPLAY

1 Mark Twain said that **womit** was one of the most important words in the German language. (Another he singled out was **damit**.)

Womit kann ich Ihnen helfen? With what can I help you?

(A preposition is a word in German you must never end a sentence with.)

2 Some other things that might get broken or not work:

Das Telefon, die Dusche, der Lift, mein Auto, mein Fotoapparat, ist kaputt.

3 If you've lost your camera, passport, car or luggage:

Ich habe meinen Fotoapparat, meinen Paß, mein Auto, mein Gepäck verloren.

If someone's stolen them:

Jemand hat meinen Fotoapparat, meinen Paß, mein Auto, mein Gepäck gestohlen.

If you want to know what it costs to clean something:

Was kostet die Reinigung?

NOW TRY IT OUT

1 Say your camera's broken and ask how much it will cost to repair it.

2 Auf der Polizeiwache

Policeman **Womit kann ich Ihnen helfen?**
You (Say someone's stolen your car.)

3 Auf der Bank

You (Say you'd like to change some traveller's cheques.)
Bank clerk **Wie viele?**
You (Say 3 for 100 – **hundert** – pounds Sterling.)

NICE TO KNOW

If you need to call the **Polizei** or even the **Feuerwehr**, you can do so from a public phone-box. Inside you'll find a small box with a lever to push to one side for the police (indicated green) or to the other for the fire-brigade (indicated red). You get a direct line, and it costs you nothing.

QUIZ

1 Problems, problems, problems! You want (1) to have your shoes repaired (2) get a coat cleaned (3) have your camera mended, and (4) report a theft to the police. These are the signs you see:

A PO FOTO-KIT   B HES ARCH CHUM
C EEZI POICH LAW   D RI IN GUNGE

Which sign do you follow up in each case, and what should it really say?

2 A funny kind of week. On Wednesday you had problems with your glasses, the lift, and your wallet. On Thursday it was with your money, the shower and the telephone. On Friday you had trouble with your camera, your car, and your passport. On the top line, write the three days of the week. Under each day fill in the names of the items you had problems with.

```
X . I . . . . . . x . . . . E . . . . . x x x . . . . . A . x x x x x
x . I . . x x x x . . . . . E x x x x x x x x x x x x . A . x x x x x
. . I . . . x x x x x . . . E . . . x x x x x x x x x x A . . . x x x
. . I . . . . . . x x . E . . x x x x x x x x . . . . A . . . . . .
```

A VERY BASIC GRAMMAR

1 NOUNS

A noun is a naming word. It names, for example, a person or an object, such as man, motorway, book, or Smith. In German, all nouns start with a capital letter. The word for 'the' depends on the gender, ie whether a noun is masculine, feminine or neuter.

der Onkel (the uncle)   **die Tasse** (the cup)   **das Buch** (the book)

Though the gender of some words is obvious (eg **der Mann**, the man or husband, **die Frau**, the wife) in most cases it is not, and the best advice is to learn the gender of each noun as you meet it.
The word for 'a' also changes according to the gender.

ein Onkel   eine Tasse   ein Buch

The words for 'my' and 'your' follow the same pattern, as does **kein** (no, or not any).

mein Onkel (my uncle)   **keine Tasse** (no cup)
dein Buch (your book)

With masculine nouns, **ein** nearly always takes the form **einen** after the verb.

Haben Sie einen Stadtplan?   Have you a plan of the city?
Es gibt einen Tennisplatz.   There is a tennis court.

Germans often pronounce **einen** in such a way as to make it difficult to decide whether they are saying **einen** or **ein**.

2 PREPOSITIONS

A preposition is a word often indicating a position, such as near, in or in front of. After a preposition, **der, die** and **das** may change their form.

das Stadion – neben dem Stadion (near the stadium)
die Bank – vor der Bank (in front of the bank)

The preposition + 'the' is sometimes shortened.

der Stadtpark – im (in + dem) Stadtpark (in the town park)

Rather than bother with the rules governing these changes, try and learn the phrases you may need.

Das Restaurant ist im Hotel.
Ich gehe zur Bank.

3 ADJECTIVES

An adjective is a word describing a noun, such as big, yellow or important. Sometimes the adjective follows the noun.

Der Wein ist gut.   The wine is good.

When it comes before the noun, it has an ending corresponding to the gender of the noun.

der Wein	**guter Wein** (good wine)
die Limonade	**gute Limonade** (good lemonade)
das Bier	**gutes Bier** (good beer)

The same characteristic endings recur elsewhere.

der Bus	**welcher Bus?** (which bus?)
die Straße	**diese Straße** (this street)
das Glas	**welches Glas?** (which glass?)

4 VERBS

A verb is a word which normally describes an action or activity, such as sing, learn or sit. The form of the verb which in English is preceded by 'to' is called the infinitive. In German the infinitive usually ends in **-en**, and there is no word for 'to'.

singen (to sing) **lernen** (to learn) **sitzen** (to sit)

The form of the verb changes according to the subject, ie the person who is doing the action.

ich singe	I sing
du singst	you sing
er/sie/es singt	he/she/it sings
wir singen	we sing
Sie singen	you sing
sie singen	they sing

The usual word for 'you' is **Sie**. Use **du** when talking to close friends, relatives, children or animals.
Ich changes form according to the role it plays in the sentence.

Ich spreche Deutsch.   I speak German.
Für mich ein Omelett.   For me an omelette.
Er gibt mir Tabletten.   He gives (to) me tablets.

Sometimes this happens in idiomatic phrases.

Hamburg gefällt mir.   I like Hamburg.

Similar changes occur with **du, er, sie, wir** and **Sie**.

Wie geht es dir?   How are you?

By putting the verb in first position, you make a question.

Haben Sie Halsschmerzen? Have you a sore throat?

Questions can also be introduced by words such as **wann?** and **wie viele?**

Wann kommt der Zug an? When does the train arrive?
Wie viele Tomaten wollen Sie? How many tomatoes do you want?

5 WORD-ORDER

Normally, the verb is the second element in the sentence (not necessarily the second word).

Ich bin auf Urlaub hier. I'm on holiday here.
Dieser Bus fährt nach Schwabing. This bus goes to Schwabing.

Sometimes, for emphasis, something other than the subject of the verb is the first element – but the verb must still be the second element.

Zum Frühstück esse ich oft ein gekochtes Ei. Literally, For breakfast eat I often a boiled egg.

The infinitive stands at the end of the sentence.

Kann man hier schwimmen? Can you swim here?

USEFUL WORDS

These are grouped under the following headings:

At the chemist's
Clothes
Eating and drinking
Emergencies
In a house
Locations and directions
Using the phone
Shopping for food
Sightseeing
Status
Travel
Weather
Numbers
Time
Days
Months

* If you want to use this word with constructions like **Ich möchte**
. . . (I would like . . .) or **Es gibt** . . . (There is . . .) then **ein** changes to
einen.

At the chemist's

a film	**ein* Film**
nappies	**Windeln**
powder	**Puder**
soap	**Seife**
tampons	**Tampons**
tissues	**Papiertaschentücher**
toilet paper	**Toilettenpapier**

Clothes

a blouse	**eine Bluse**
a bra	**ein* BH (Büstenhalter)**
a dress	**ein Kleid**

a hat	ein* Hut
a jacket	eine Jacke
a jogging suit	ein* Jogginganzug
pants (men's)	eine Unterhose
pants (women's)	ein* Slip
a raincoat	ein* Regenmantel
a shirt	ein Hemd
a pair of shoes	ein Paar Schuhe
a skirt	ein* Rock
socks	Socken
a suit	ein* Anzug
sunglasses	eine Sonnenbrille
a swimming costume	ein* Badeanzug
tights	eine Strumpfhose
trainers	Turnschuhe
trousers	eine Hose

Eating and drinking

I'm thirsty	ich habe Durst/ich bin durstig
I'm hungry	ich habe Hunger/ich bin hungrig
a set meal	ein Gedeck
take-away	zum Mitnehmen
a knife	ein Messer
a fork	eine Gabel
a spoon	ein* Löffel
a plate	ein* Teller
the wine-list	die Weinliste
mineral water	Mineralwasser
decaffeinated	koffeinfrei

Emergencies

contact lenses	Kontaktlinsen
an umbrella	ein* Regenschirm
a button	ein* Knopf
a safety pin	eine Sicherheitsnadel
a breakdown	eine Panne
a strike	ein* Streik
help!	Hilfe!
quick!	schnell!
stop!	Halt!

In a house

the bathroom	das Badezimmer
to have a bath	baden
to shower	duschen

a towel	ein Handtuch
a bedroom	ein Schlafzimmer
the cellar	der Keller
the central heating	die Zentralheizung
a cupboard	ein* Schrank
the dining-room	das Eßzimmer
drinking water	Trinkwasser
the floor, storey	der Stock, die Etage
the garden	der Garten
a guest room	ein Gästezimmer
the hall	der Flur
the kitchen	die Küche
the lounge	das Wohnzimmer

Locations and directions

above	über
behind	hinter
between	zwischen
next door	nebenan
opposite	gegenüber
underneath	unter
cross the bridge	gehen Sie über die Brücke
get off, get out	steigen Sie ... aus
past the cathedral	am Dom vorbei
the direction	die Richtung

Using the phone

the code	die Vorwahlnummer
the extension	der Nebenanschluß
I'd like to speak to Mr Brown	ich möchte Herrn Braun sprechen
hold the line	bleiben Sie am Apparat
it's engaged	es ist besetzt
there's no reply	niemand meldet sich
who's speaking	wer ist da?
speaking	am Apparat
goodbye	auf Wiederhören

Shopping for food

frozen food	Tiefkühlkost
tinned food	Lebensmittelkonserven
a bag of ...	eine Tüte ...
a bottle of ...	eine Flasche ...
a packet of ...	eine Packung ...
a tin of ...	eine Büchse .../eine Dose ...

Sightseeing

the beach	der Strand
a castle	ein Schloß/eine Burg
a church	eine Kirche
an exhibition	eine Ausstellung
a fountain	ein* Brunnen
a harbour	ein* Hafen
an island	eine Insel
a lake	ein* See
the sea	die See
a mountain	ein* Berg
a pedestrian area	eine Fußgängerzone
shade	Schatten
entrance free	Eintritt frei
a guide	ein* Führer
a guide book	ein* Taschenführer
a guided tour	eine Führung
sold out	ausgebucht

Status

married	verheiratet
divorced	geschieden
single	ledig
a widow	Witwe
a widower	Witwer

Travel

all directions	alle Richtungen
other directions	andere Richtungen
give way	Vorfahrt beachten
the crossroads	die Kreuzung
a warning triangle	ein Warndreieck
a parking meter	eine Parkuhr
a puncture	eine Reifenpanne
a service station	eine Werkstatt
a driving licence	ein* Führerschein
an insurance certificate	ein* Versicherungsschein
car rental	Auto-Vermietung
entry	Eingang/Einfahrt
exit	Ausgang/Ausfahrt
connecting services	Anschluß/Verbindungen
left luggage	Gepäckaufbewahrung
a waiting room	ein Wartezimmer
the restaurant car	der Speisewagen
a sleeper	ein* Schlafwagen
a ferry	eine Fähre

Weather

cold	**kalt**
warm	**warm**
hot	**heiß**
sun	**Sonne**
rain	**Regen**
fog	**Nebel**
hail	**Hagel**
snow	**Schnee**
ice	**Eis**
wind	**Wind**

Numbers

0	**null**	21	**einundzwanzig**
1	**eins**	22	**zweiundzwanzig**
2	**zwei**	23	**dreiundzwanzig**
3	**drei**	24	**vierundzwanzig**
4	**vier**	25	**fünfundzwanzig**
5	**fünf**	26	**sechsundzwanzig**
6	**sechs**	27	**siebenundzwanzig**
7	**sieben**	28	**achtundzwanzig**
8	**acht**	29	**neunundzwanzig**
9	**neun**	30	**dreißig**
10	**zehn**	40	**vierzig**
11	**elf**	50	**fünfzig**
12	**zwölf**	60	**sechzig**
13	**dreizehn**	70	**siebzig**
14	**vierzehn**	80	**achtzig**
15	**fünfzehn**	90	**neunzig**
16	**sechzehn**	100	**hundert**
17	**siebzehn**	200	**zweihundert**
18	**achtzehn**	1000	**tausend**
19	**neunzehn**		
20	**zwanzig**		

Instead of **zwei, zwo** is often said – especially on the telephone – to avoid confusion with **drei**.

Time

The twenty-four-hour clock

Um ein / zwei / drei . . . / vierundzwanzig Uhr fünf . . . neunundfünfzig.

Alternatively:

Um zehn Minuten vor elf (At ten to eleven)
Um fünfundzwanzig Minuten vor drei (At twenty-five to three)

Um Viertel nach sieben (At a quarter past seven)

NB **Um halb sechs** (At half past *five*)

Days

Monday	**Montag**
Tuesday	**Dienstag**
Wednesday	**Mittwoch**
Thursday	**Donnerstag**
Friday	**Freitag**
Saturday	**Samstag** or **Sonnabend**
Sunday	**Sonntag**
on Mondays	**montags**
on working days	**werktags**

Months

January	**Januar**
February	**Februar**
March	**März**
April	**April**
May	**Mai**
June	**Juni**
July	**Juli**
August	**August**
September	**September**
October	**Oktober**
November	**November**
December	**Dezember**

ANSWERS

LEKTION 1

Now try it out

1 Bitte! / Hallo!
2 Bitte schön? Ein Bier und ein Mineralwasser.
3 Ein Kännchen Kaffee, ein Bier und zwei Glas Rotwein.
4 Ein großes Bier. Wo sind die Toiletten?
5 Bitte! / Hallo! Bitte schön? Kaffee, bitte. Eine Tasse oder ein
   Kännchen? Ein Kännchen. Sonst noch etwas? Ein Glas
   Weißwein und zwei Glas Orangensaft. Zahlen, bitte!

Quiz

1 Thirsty? A **Tomatensaft** B **Orangensaft** C **Champagner**
   D **Tee** E **Kaffee** F **Apfelsaft** G **Milch** H **Weißwein**
   I **Sekt** J **Limonade** K **Mineralwasser** L **Kognak**
   M **Schnaps** N **Wasser** O **Schokolade** P **Rotwein**
   Q **Whisky**
2 All mixed up. D **Guten Tag! Bitte schön?** B **Ein Bier, bitte.**
   F **Ein großes oder ein kleines?** H **Ein kleines.**
   A **Sonst noch etwas?** I **Ja! Kaffee, bitte!** C **Eine Tasse oder
   ein Kännchen?** E **Ein Kännchen.** G **Zahlen, bitte!**

LEKTION 2

Action

A aspirin B bread C to change cheques
A list of hotels B plan of city C list of camping sites

Now try it out

1 A **Das Postamt? Hier geradeaus, und dann nach links** B is
   correct C **Sie wollen das Fremdenverkehrsamt? Gehen Sie
   hier immer geradeaus.**
2 **Auf der Straße. Entschuldigen Sie bitte. Wo ist hier das
   Fremdenverkehrsamt? In der Königstraße. Hier geradeaus.
   Die erste links. Danke schön! Bitte schön!**
3 **Im Fremdenverkehrsamt. Guten Tag! Bitte schön? Guten
   Tag! Ich hätte gern eine Hotelliste. Bitte schön. Sonst noch
   etwas? Was gibt es hier in Hamburg zu sehen? Allerlei!
   Haben Sie eine Broschüre? Natürlich. Bitte schön! Danke
   schön!**

Quiz

1 Pair them up. 1D 2E 3A 4B 5F 6C
2 All squashed up. 'Guten Tag!' 'Guten Tag! Was gibt es hier in
   Nürnberg zu sehen?' 'Bitte schön. Eine Liste der
   Sehenswürdigkeiten. Sonst noch etwas?' 'Ich hätte gern eine
   Liste der Campingplätze.'

LEKTION 3

Now try it out

1 Im Hotel. Guten Tag! Guten Tag! Haben Sie Zimmer frei? Ja,
   natürlich. Was für Zimmer möchten Sie? Zwei
   Doppelzimmer und ein Einzelzimmer, mit Dusche. Für wie
   viele Nächte? Zwei Nächte. Was kostet das? Ein
   Doppelzimmer kostet hundert Mark pro Nacht und ein
   Einzelzimmer kostet achtzig. Ist das mit Frühstück?

2 Auf dem Campingplatz. Guten Abend! Haben Sie Platz frei?
   Ja. Für wie lange? Eine Nacht. Und wie viele Personen,
   bitte? Drei Erwachsene und zwei Kinder. Haben Sie einen
   Wohnwagen? Nein, wir haben drei Zelte. Gut. Ihr Name,
   bitte?

Quiz

1 A lost letter. Missing letter – e. A **Hotel** B **Pension**
   C **Empfang** D **Rechnung** E **Dusche** F **frei** G **Schlüssel**
   H **Wohnwagen** I **Zelt** J **Einzelzimmer** K **Doppelzimmer**
   L **besetzt** M **Reservierung** N **Erwachsene** O **Kinder**
2 Mr Smartt. 1B 2A 3D 4E 5C

LEKTION 4

Now try it out

1 Zweimal Bratwurst mit Pommes frites und Mayo.
2 Im Schnellimbiß. Was möchten Sie? Eine Frankfurter. Mit
   Ketchup? Nein, mit Senf!
3 In der Café-Konditorei. Bitte schön? Dreimal Apfelkuchen.
   Mit Sahne? Zweimal mit Sahne, einmal ohne Sahne.

Quiz

1 What a mess. A **Bratwurst**
   B **Schokoladenkuchen** C **Erdbeereis**
   D **Schwarzwälder Kirschtorte** E **Himbeertorte**
   F **Vanilleeis**

2 A mean menu.   If you want anything with your **Himbeereis**,
   then it would be **Sahne**. If you're keen on cream you could have
   Sahne with your **Sahnetorte**, too. But not your **Bratwurst –
   Senf** or **Ketchup** might go down better.

LEKTION 5

Now try it out

1 Ich heiße John. Ich bin Engländer. Ich bin aus Manchester.
   Ich heiße Heather. Ich bin Schottin. Ich bin aus Glasgow.
   Ich heiße . . . Ich bin . . . Ich bin aus . . .
2 Im Restaurant. Guten Abend! Guten Abend! Wie geht's?
   Danke, gut! Und Ihnen?
3 Im Hotel. Wie heißen Sie? Ich heiße / mein Name ist . . . Ich
   bin aus . . . Mein Name ist Wolfgang. Bist du Deutscher? Ja –
   ich bin aus Köln. Bitte? Köln – auf englisch, Cologne. Are you
   English? Auf deutsch, bitte!

Quiz

1 On course? Of course! Ich heiße . . . und ich bin A Frankfurter
   B **Engländer** C Amerikanerin D Hamburger E Berlinerin
   F **Frankfurterin** G Deutscher H **Amerikaner**
   I **Engländerin** J Schottin K Deutsche L **Schotte**
   M Berliner N Hamburgerin
2 Some conversation! 'Guten Tag!' 'Guten Tag!' 'Wie geht's?'
   'Gut, danke! Und Ihnen?' 'Gut danke!' 'Sind Sie Deutscher?'
   'Ja, ich bin Deutscher. Ich heiße Boris Becker. Sind Sie
   Engländerin?' 'Ja, ich bin aus London.' 'Wie heißen Sie,
   bitte?' 'Ich heiße Prinzessin Diana.'

LEKTION 6

Now try it out

1 Einige Bananen, bitte!
2 Hundert Gramm Aufschnitt, bitte!
3 Auf dem Markt. Bitte schön? Was darf es sein? Was kosten
   die Tomaten? Fünf Mark das Kilo. Ein Pfund, bitte. Diese?
   Nein, kleinere! Sonst noch etwas? Haben Sie Himbeeren?

Quiz

1   Find the food

```
L L T O M A T E N T W I
R E H O A B E N T L N N
E F K I R S D I E R E E
K P E C A B N I H B K R
N A N N I H U I U E N E
E P A R C N M A F I I E
N N S R B R S R I H B
A E F C E T H E E G C D
N U U E N N D K P E S R
A P R I K O S E N M I E
B E E N E K I R S C U H
N W E I ß B R O T E N P
```

Message: **Wir haben leider keine Pfirsiche und keine Kirschen.**

2   Really Smartt.   A **Tomaten sind rot.**   B **Gras ist grün.**
    C **Der Himmel ist blau.**   D **Bananen sind gelb.**
    E **Pumpernickel ist schwarz.**   F **Weißbrot ist weiß.**
    G **Graubrot ist grau.**

LEKTION 7

Now try it out

1   **Welcher Bus fährt zum Stadtzentrum?**
2   **Zweimal Marktplatz, bitte!**
3   **Entschuldigen Sie! Wie komme ich am besten zum Dom?**
    Geradeaus, und die dritte Straße rechts.
4   **Wann ist das Museum geöffnet? Von 11.00 Uhr bis 17.00 Uhr.**
    Welche Straßenbahn fährt zum Museum? Linie dreizehn!
    Wo ist die nächste Haltestelle?

Quiz

1   Which way's that?   A **Die zweite Straße rechts.**   B **Die dritte
    Straße links.**   C **Die erste Straße rechts.**   D **Die zweite
    Straße links.**   E **Die erste Straße links.**   F **Die dritte Straße
    rechts.**
2   When? How? Where?   A **Am Dienstag fährt er mit dem Bus
    zum Museum.**   B **Am Freitag fährt er mit dem Auto zum
    Panoptikum.**   C **Am Donnerstag fährt er mit der U-Bahn**

zum Stadtzentrum. D Am Mittwoch fährt er mit der
Straßenbahn zum Marktplatz. E Am Montag fährt er mit
der S-Bahn zum Dom. F Am Sonntag fährt er mit dem Zug
zum Schloß. G Am Samstag geht er zu Fuß zur Post.

LEKTION 8

Now try it out

1 Zwanzig Liter Super, bitte!
2 Für fünfundvierzig Mark. Super!
3 Die Batterie prüfen, bitte!
4 An der Tankstelle. Bitte schön? Volltanken, bitte! Super? Ja,
   bleifrei. Bitte schön! Was macht das? Das macht
   fünfunddreißig Mark. Die Reifen prüfen, bitte.

Quiz

1 Tongue-tied? **Guten Abend! Volltanken, bitte! Bleifrei. Was**
   macht das? Die Reifen prüfen, bitte!
2 Quality cars. A **Volkswagen** B **Mercedes Benz**
   C **Bayerische Motorenwerke / BMW**

LEKTION 9

Now try it out

1 Fünf nach Stuttgart. Zwei Erwachsene und drei Kinder.
2 Einfach. Zweiter Klasse.
3 Ist das der Zug nach Köln?
4 Ist hier frei?
5 Am Fahrkartenschalter. Wann fährt der nächste Zug nach
   Nürnberg, bitte? Um 14.25 Uhr. Muß ich umsteigen? Nein, er
   fährt direkt. Von welchem Gleis?

Quiz

1 Ooops! 3 **Wohin, bitte?** E **Nach Hannover.** 5 **Einmal?**
   B **Nein, zweimal.** 2 **Einfach, oder hin und zurück?**
   C **Hin und zurück.** 4 **Welcher Klasse?** A **Zweiter Klasse.**
   6 **Wann fährt der nächste Zug nach Hannover?**
   D **Um 16.39 Uhr.** 1 **Wann kommt er an?** F **Um 18.25 Uhr.**
2 Some trip! Hamburg – Lübeck – Hannover – Düsseldorf – Köln –
   Frankfurt-am-Main – Stuttgart – Nürnberg – München – Berlin

LEKTION 10

Now try it out

1 Ich bin . . . (Look up your job in a dictionary!)
2 Das ist mein Mann. Er ist Ingenieur. Und Sie? Ich bin
   Ärztin.
3 Ist hier frei? Bitte schön! Gefällt Ihnen die Konferenz? Ja,
   sehr. Trinken Sie gern Löwenbräu?
4 Hamburg ist schön, nicht wahr? Ja, Hamburg gefällt mir.
   Sind Sie auf Urlaub hier? Nein, ich bin geschäftlich hier.

Quiz

1 All mixed up.   1C 2A 3D 4E 5B
2 Mum's the word.

MISSING MESSAGE: **Meine Großmutter. Sie ist Ringerin von
Beruf.**

LEKTION 11

Now try it out

1 Gibt es hier ein Hallenbad?
2 Ich möchte einen Liegestuhl mieten. Was kostet das?
3 Ich möchte ein Windsurfbrett für einen Tag mieten. Wollen
   Sie eine Anzahlung?
4 At the ski hire shop. Bitte schön? Ich möchte ein Paar Skier
   mieten. Ja, für wie lange? Was kostet das? Zwanzig Mark
   pro Tag. Für drei Tage. Kein Problem! Ihr Name, bitte, und
   Ihre Adresse? Mein Name ist . . . Pension Friedegg.

Quiz

1 Not quite right. 1C 2E 3A 4B 5D
2 Nice girls. A **Frankreich** B **Die Schweiz** C **Jugoslawien**
   D **Österreich** E **Italien** F **Spanien** G **Deutschland.**

LEKTION 12

Now try it out

1 Drei Postkarten zu sechzig Pfennig und vier zu fünfzig
   Pfennig. Was bin ich Ihnen schuldig?
2 Was kosten diese Postkarten? Eine Mark das Stück. Zu
   teuer! Haben Sie keine anderen?
3 Auf der Post. Was kostet eine Postkarte nach Schottland?
   Sechzig Pfennig. Zehn Briefmarken zu sechzig Pfennig.
   Bitte schön! Ist hier in der Nähe ein Briefkasten?

Quiz

1 Some titles! A **Welt** / world B **Bunte** / colourful
   C **Zeitung** / newspaper D **Spiegel** / mirror E **Bild** / picture
   F **Stern** / star.
2 Careful! **Schottland ist nicht England! Schottland und
   England sind in Großbritannien!**

LEKTION 13

Now try it out

1 Haben Sie einen Tisch für vier?
2 Im Restaurant. Bitte! / Hallo! Bitte schön? Das Menü / Die
   Speisekarte, bitte! Bitte schön! Ratsherrenschmaus – was ist
   das? Das ist Roastbeef und Schweinebraten auf Graubrot.
   Ein Kalbsschnitzel mit Nudeln, bitte. Und zu trinken? Ein
   Glas Weißwein.

Quiz

1 Not quite right. **Haben Sie einen Tisch für drei? Hallo! Die
   Speisekarte, bitte. Kalbsschnitzel mit Nudeln. Eine Flasche
   Rotwein. Zahlen, bitte!**
2 Chopped-up meats. A **Rindfleisch** B **Schweinefleisch**
   C **Hammelfleisch** D **Kalbfleisch.**

LEKTION 14

Now try it out

1 Beim Arzt. Guten Tag, Herr Doktor! Guten Tag! Was fehlt
   Ihnen? Meine Nase tut weh und ich habe Fieber. Haben Sie
   Halsschmerzen? Ja, und Durchfall.
2 In der Apotheke. Haben Sie etwas gegen Sonnenbrand? Ja,
   eine Salbe? Danke schön. Was kostet das?

Quiz

1 Come again? Guten Tag, Herr Doktor! Mir ist schlecht. Ich
   bin krank. Meine Brust tut weh und ich habe
   Halsschmerzen!
2 Sounds painful. A **Halsschmerzen** B **Kopfschmerzen**
   C **Durchfall** D **Magenschmerzen** E **Zahnschmerzen**
   F **Verstopfung.**

LEKTION 15

Now try it out

1 Mein Fotoapparat ist kaputt. Was kostet die Reparatur?
2 Auf der Polizeiwache. Womit kann ich Ihnen helfen?
   Jemand hat mein Auto gestohlen.
3 Auf der Bank. Ich möchte Reiseschecks wechseln. Wie
   viele? Drei zu hundert Pfund Sterling.

Quiz

1 Problems, problems, problems! A **FOTO-OPTIK**
   B **SCHUHMACHER** C **POLIZEIWACHE**
   D **REINIGUNG.** (1)=B, (2)=D, (3)=A, (4)=C.
2 A funny kind of week.

```
×MITTWOCH×DONNERSTAG×××FREITAG×××××
×LIFT××××DUSCHE×××××××××××PAß×××××
BRILLE×××××TELEFON×××××××××××AUTO×××
BRIEFTASCHE××GELD×××××××FOTOAPPARAT
```

GERMAN–ENGLISH VOCABULARY

	aber but, however
die	**Abfahrt** the departure
	alle all, everybody
	allerlei all kinds of, all kinds of things
	alles everything
	am besten in the best way
das	**Amt** the office
	an (am) at, to
	andere other, others
die	**Ankunft** the arrival
die	**Anzahlung** the deposit
der	**Apfel** the apple
die	**Apotheke** the pharmacist's
die	**Aprikose** the apricot
der	**Arzt (die Ärztin)** the doctor
	auch also
	auf on

die	**Bäckerei** the baker's, bread shop
die	**Bahn** the way, track
mit der	**Bahn** by rail
der	**Bahnhof** the railway station
die	**Bedienung** the service
	bei at, at the house of, at the shop of
der	**Berg** the mountain
der	**Beruf** the job, profession
	besetzt full, reserved, engaged
	billig cheap; **billiger** cheaper
ich	**bin** I am
die	**Birne** the pear
	bis until
ein	**bißchen** a bit
du	**bist** you are
	bitte please; **bitte schön** please do, go ahead, there you are, don't mention it
	bleiben to remain; **bleiben Sie** remain
	bleifrei lead-free
der	**Blumenladen** the flower-shop
die	**Bohnen** the beans
	brauchen to need
der	**Brief** the letter

der	**Briefkasten** the letter-box
die	**Briefmarke** the postage-stamp
die	**Brieftasche** the wallet
die	**Brille** the spectacles
das	**Brot** the bread
das	**Brötchen** the roll of bread

	da there; **da drüben** over there
die	**Dame** the lady
	danke, danke schön thank you
	dann then
	das that; **das kostet, das macht** that costs
	dazu in addition
	der, die, das the
	deutsch German
	Deutschland Germany
	dich you
	dies this; **diese** these
	dir to you
	doch yes
der	**Dom** the cathedral
das	**Doppelzimmer** the double room
die	**Drogerie** the drugstore
	du you
die	**Dusche** the shower

das	**Ei** the egg
	ein, eine a, one
	einfach simple, a single ticket
	einige some, a few
	einmal one, once
das	**Einzelzimmer** the single room
das	**Eis** the ice-cream
die	**Eisenbahn** the railway
der	**Empfang** the reception
der	**Entwerter** the cancelling machine
	er he, it
die	**Erdbeere** the strawberry
die	**Erkältung** the cold
	erster Klasse first class
der	**Erwachsene** the adult
	es it; **es gefällt mir** I like it; **es gibt** there is, are; **es tut weh** it hurts
	etwas something

	fahren to go, travel
der	**Fahrkartenschalter** the ticket office
der	**Fahrplan** the time-table
das	**Fahrrad** the bicycle
die	**Fahrt** the journey, trip
er	**fährt** he goes, travels
Sie	**finden** you find
der	**Fischladen** the fishmonger's
die	**Flasche** the bottle
das	**Fleisch** the meat
die	**Frau** the woman, wife, Mrs
das	**Fräulein** the young woman, Miss
	frei free, vacant
das	**Fremdenverkehrsamt** the Tourist Information Office
das	**Fundbüro** the lost-property office
	für for; **für 30 DM** 30 marks worth; **für wie lange?** for how long?

ich	**gebe** I give, am giving
	geben to give
	gebraten fried, roasted
(es)	**gefällt mir** I like (it); **wie gefällt Ihnen . . . / wie gefällt dir . . .** how do you like . . . ?
	gegen against, for
ich	**gehe** I go, am going
	gehen to go; **gehen Sie** go; **gehen Sie gern . . . ?** do you like going . . . ?
	gekocht boiled
das	**Geld** the money
das	**Gemüse** the vegetable, vegetables
	geöffnet open, opened
das	**Gepäck** the luggage
	geradeaus straight on
	gern, gerne willingly; **trinken Sie gern . . . ?** do you like drinking . . . ?
	geschäftlich on business
	geschlossen closed
hat's	**geschmeckt?** did you like it? did it taste good?
	gestohlen stolen
das	**Getränk** the drink
es	**gibt** there is
	gleich straight away
das	**Gleis** the track, platform
	grau grey
	groß big
	grün green
	gut good

ich	**habe** I have; **haben** to have; **haben Sie . . . ?** have you got . . . ?	
die	**Haltestelle** the stop	
ich	**hätte gern** I would like	
	heiß hot	
ich	**heiße** I am called	
	helfen to help	
der	**Herr** the gentleman, Mr	
	heute today	
	hier here	
	hin und zurück a return ticket	

	ich I	
	Ihnen (to) you	
	Ihr your	
die	**Imbißstube** the snackbar	
	immer geradeaus keep going straight on	
	ist is	

	ja yes	
	jeden Tag every day	
	jemand someone	

	kalt cold	
	kann can	
das	**Kännchen** the pot	
die	**Kartoffeln** the potatoes	
der	**Käse** the cheese	
die	**Kasse** the cash desk	
	kaufen to buy	
	kein, keine no, not any	
das	**Kind** the child	
die	**Kirsche** the cherry	
	klein small, little; **kleiner** smaller	
die	**Kneipe** the pub	
ich	**komme** I come, am coming	
	kommen to come	
ich	**komme . . . an** I arrive, am arriving; **er kommt . . . an** he / it arrives	
	können to be able	
	Kopfschmerzen a headache	
	kosten to cost	
es	**kostet** it costs	
	krank poorly, sick	

die	**Küche** cooking, the kitchen
der	**Kuchen** the cake

der	**Laden** the shop
	Lebensmittel the food
	links left, on the left; **auf der linken Seite** on the left-hand side
die	**Luft** the air

	machen to make, do; **das macht 5 DM** that comes to 5 DM
das	**Mädchen** the girl
	Magenschmerzen stomach-ache
	man one, you
der	**Mann** the man, husband
der	**Markt** the market; **der Marktplatz** the market-place
	mehr more
	Mehrwertsteuer enthalten VAT included
	mein, meine my
	mich me
	mieten to hire
	mir to me; **mir gefällt . . .** I like; **mir geht's (nicht) gut** I'm (not) well / **mir ist heiß** I'm hot; **mir ist kalt** I'm cold; **mir ist schlecht** I feel sick
	mit with
ich	**möchte** I would like
ich	**muß** I must

	nach to, after; **nach rechts** to the right
der	**nächste** the next, nearest
die	**Nacht** the night
in der	**Nähe** in the neighbourhood
	natürlich naturally, of course
	neben next to, near
	nehmen Sie take
	nein no
	nicht not; **nicht wahr?** isn't that so?
der	**Nichtraucher** the non-smoker
	niedrig low
	noch ein Bier another beer; **noch etwas** some more

das	**Obst** the fruit
	oder or
	Öffnungszeiten opening hours
	ohne without

ein	**Paar** a pair
der	**Paß** the passport
der	**Pfirsich** the peach
der	**Pilz** the mushroom
der	**Platz** the place, square, space, room
die	**Polizeiwache** the police-station
	prüfen to check

	radfahren to cycle
der	**Rastplatz** the resting-place
der	**Raucher** the smoker
die	**Rechnung** the bill
	rechts right, on the right; **auf der rechten Seite** on the right-hand side
der	**Reifen** the tyre
die	**Reinigung** the cleaner's
das	**Rezept** the prescription
	rot red
die	**Rundfahrt** the round trip, circular tour

die	**Sahne** the cream
der	**Schinken** the ham
	schlecht bad; **mir ist schlecht** I feel sick
das	**Schloß** the castle
der	**Schlüssel** the key
der	**Schnellimbiß** the snackbar
	schön pretty, beautiful, nice
der	**Schuh** the shoe
	schwarz black
	schwimmen to swim
die	**See** the sea
	sehen to see
die	**Sehenswürdigkeiten** the sights
	sehr very
	sein to be
die	**Seite** the side, page
die	**Selbstbedienung** the self-service
der	**Senf** the mustard

	Sie	you
	sie	she, they
	sind	are
	skifahren	to ski
	so	like that
die	**Sonnenkrem**	the sun-tan cream
	sonst noch etwas?	anything else?
die	**Speisekarte**	the menu
	spielen	to play
	sprechen	to speak
das	**Stadion**	the stadium
der	**Stadtplan**	the map of the town
das	**Stadtzentrum**	the town-centre
die	**Stelle**	the place
die	**Straße**	the street
das	**Stück**	the piece
die	**Stunde**	the hour
der	**Supermarkt**	the supermarket
die	**Suppe**	the soup

der	**Tag**	the day; **... am Tag** ... per day
die	**Tankstelle**	the filling station
	tanzen	to dance
die	**Tasse**	the cup
	teuer	dear, expensive
der	**Tisch**	the table
die	**Torte**	the tart, flan

	übernachten	to spend the night
	um ... Uhr	at ... o'clock
	und	and
	unterwegs	on the way

	verboten	forbidden, not allowed
der	**Verkehr**	the traffic
	verloren	lost
	viel	much; **vielen Dank** many thanks
	volltanken	to fill up
	vom (von dem)	from the, of the
	von	from, of
	vor	before, in front of, ago

wandern to hike, walk

wann? when?

was what; **was darf es sein?** what would you like?; **was fehlt Ihnen?** what's the matter?; **was für . . . ?** what kind of . . . ? **was kostet das?** what does that cost?; **was macht das?** what does that cost?; **was sind Sie von Beruf?** what's your job?

das **Wasser** the water

wechseln to exchange

weiß white

welcher, welche, welches which

wenig little; **weniger** less

wie how; **wie bitte?** I beg your pardon; **wie geht's** how are you? **wie heißen Sie?** what's your name?; **wie lange?** how long?

wieviel? how much?; **wie viele?** how many?

du **willst** you want

wir we

wo where

die **Woche** the week

woher where from

wohin where to

der **Wohnwagen** the caravan

wollen to want to, wish; **wollen Sie?** do you want, wish

womit with what

zahlen to pay

das **Zelt** the tent

das **Zimmer** the room

zu to

der **Zug** the train

zum (zu dem), zur (zu der) to the

zurück back

zusammen together